ACHIEVING EXTRAORDINARY ENDS:
AN ESSAY ON CREATIVITY

# Achieving Extraordinary Ends: An Essay on Creativity

Sharon Bailin

*Faculty of Education,
University of Manitoba, Winnipeg*

1988

KLUWER ACADEMIC PUBLISHERS

Dordrecht / Boston / Lancaster

**Library of Congress Cataloging-in-Publication Data**

Bailin, Sharon.
  Achieving extraordinary ends: an essay on creativity / Sharon Bailin.
     p.    cm.
  Bibliography: p.
  Includes index.
  ISBN 90-247-3674-9
  1. Creative ability.  2. Creation (literary, artistic, etc.)  I. Title.
BF408.B33      1988
153.3´5--dc19




Published by Kluwer Academic Publishers,
P.O. Box 17, 3300 AA Dordrecht, The Netherlands

Kluwer Academic Publishers incorporates the publishing programmes of
D. Reidel, Martinus Nijhoff, Dr. W. Junk and MTP Press

Sold and distributed in the U.S.A. and Canada
by Kluwer Academic Publishers,
101 Philip Drive, Norwell, MA 02061, U.S.A.

In all other countries, sold and distributed
by Kluwer Academic Publishers Group,
P.O. Box 322, 3300 AH Dordrecht, The Netherlands




All rights reserved.
© 1988 by Kluwer Academic Publishers
No part of the material protected by this copyright notice may be reproduced or
utilized in any form or by any means, electronic or mechanical
including photocopying, recording or by any information storage and
retrieval system, without written permission from the copyright owner.

Printed in The Netherlands.

To the memory of my father
Harry Carl Goldstein

# TABLE OF CONTENTS

| | | |
|---|---|---|
| | ACKNOWLEDGEMENTS | ix |
| | INTRODUCTION | 1 |
| | The Context | 1 |
| | The Contemporary View | 2 |
| | Problems with the Contemporary View | 4 |
| I | ORIGINALITY | 7 |
| | Originality, Novelty, and Continuity | 8 |
| | Art | 10 |
| | Science and Technology | 18 |
| | Mathematics | 23 |
| | Problem-Solving and Originality in Everyday Life | 24 |
| | Summary | 31 |
| II | VALUE | 33 |
| | Value in Art | 35 |
| | Value in Science | 49 |
| | Art and Science | 54 |
| | Summary | 59 |
| III | PRODUCT, PROCESS, PERSON | 61 |
| | Product | 61 |
| | Process | 64 |
| | Persons | 79 |
| | Summary | 84 |
| IV | RULES, SKILLS, AND KNOWLEDGE | 87 |
| | Rules and Art | 88 |
| | Rules and Science | 98 |
| | Knowledge and Problem-Solving | 104 |
| | Summary | 105 |
| V | THE SOMETHING MORE | 109 |
| | Art and the Something More | 110 |
| | Science and the Something More | 120 |
| | Generation and Criticism | 121 |
| | Emotion and Attitude | 126 |
| | Fostering Creativity | 128 |
| | INDEX | 135 |

# ACKNOWLEDGEMENTS

I would like to express my sincere appreciation to the following individuals for their helpful comments on my ideas and my writings: Rodney Clifton, Dianne Common, Richard Courtney, Robert Ennis, Jagdish Hattiangadi, Arthur I. Miller, John Morgan, Richard Paul, David Perkins, and David Savan. I am indebted to my colleagues at the Ontario Institute for Studies in Education, at York University, and at the University of Manitoba for their sound advice and unfailing support. My graduate students at the University of Manitoba deserve a note of thanks for lively discussion of the issues contained herein. For their advice and constant encouragement of my work I would like to thank J. Anthony Blair and Stanley Tweyman. I am particularly indebted to Harvey Siegel for his always insightful discussion of the arguments and his detailed reading of and commentary on the manuscript. His criticisms and suggestions for improvement, as well as his support, have been invaluable. And a special thank you must go to Ian Winchester — as mentor, colleague, critic, and friend. Our discussions over the years, his comments on my writings, and his constant encouragement have been significant for me in the development of this work. Finally, thank you to Jeremy and to Ailey for being there for me.

I would like to acknowledge the assistance of grants from the Social Sciences and Humanities Research Council of Canada.

This book is based, in part, on some of my previous writings: "Creativity and Skill," in J. Bishop, J. Lochhead, and D.N. Perkins, eds., *Thinking: The Second International Conference* (Hillsdale, N.J.: Erlbaum, 1987); "Critical and Creative Thinking," *Informal Logic* 9 (1987); "Creativity or Quality: A Deceptive Choice," *Journal of Educational Thought* 21, 1 (1987); "Art and Science: Creation or Discovery?" in D. DeLuca, ed., *Essays on Creativity and Science* (Honolulu: Hawaii Council of Teachers of English, 1986); "On Originality," *Interchange* 16, 1 (1985); "Can There Be Creativity Without Creation?" *Interchange* 15, 2 (1984). I would like to thank the publishers for permission to use parts of these articles.

# INTRODUCTION

CREATIVITY HAS become a popular slogan in contemporary education and society. We are urged continually to be creative with respect to all our endeavours—to be creative writers, creative cooks, creative teachers, creative thinkers, creative lovers. Ascribing creativity has become one of the principal means of praising, approving, and commending.

Yet in the process of becoming a universal term of positive evaluation, the concept of creativity has tended to lose its connection with its origins. We have forgotten that creativity has to do with creating, that it is connected with great achievements and quality productions. And as a consequence of this lapse of memory, most attempts to foster creativity in educational practice have been misleading at best and dangerous at worst. We have come to settle for the encouragement of certain personality traits at the expense of the encouragement of significant achievement—and this in the name of creativity. If we are not clear about what is meant by creativity, we may end up sacrificing creativity precisely in the process of trying to foster it. This book is an attempt to be clear about creativity.

## *The Context*

For the poet is an airy thing, a winged and a holy thing; and he cannot make poetry until he becomes inspired and goes out of his senses and no mind is left in him.

Plato[1]

If creativity and its growth are to be viewed scientifically, creativity must be defined in a way that permits objective observation and measurement...

E. Paul Torrance[2]

The concept of creativity which is reflected in contemporary educational theory and practice is of relatively recent origin. In previous centuries, creativity tended to be viewed in terms of divine inspiration or individual genius—neither source admitting of the possibility of external intervention. The present century, the latter half in particular, has been witness, however, to attempts to deal with this concept in a new way—scientifically. This new attitude to creativity was given its greatest impetus by Guilford in 1950. In his address to the American Psychological Association in that year, Guilford pointed out what he considered to be a shocking neglect of the entire area of creativity in the psychological literature,[3] and his work inspired a vast amount of research on the subject. Some of the research was aimed at investigating the nature of the thinking process involved in creativity, for example Guilford's own factorial analysis of cognitive traits. The identification and description of creative individuals was the focus of other investigations, such as those of Torrance. Yet other studies, notably those of MacKinnon and Barron, attempted an analysis of personality and environmental determinants.[4]

Research of this type entails a very different way of viewing creativity from the previous one, focussing not on extraordinary achievement but rather on process. Once creativity is seen as a specific process or mode of thought, the possibility arises that it can be taught (or at least fostered), and so creativity research has had considerable influence on educational theory and practice. Torrance, Parnes, and De Bono, for example,[5] have proposed principles and methods for encouraging creativity and have been in the forefront of a growing number of psychologists and educators who view the fostering of creativity as a fundamental educational goal. And the educational scene, particularly in the United States, has experienced a burgeoning of courses designed specifically to promote creative thinking. The field of arts education has also been influenced significantly by creativity research, and the development of creativity has been stressed as a goal by educators in many of the arts. This emphasis on creativity is evident, as well, in pedagogical approaches to disciplines other than the arts—for example in stressing the need for divergent thinking and imagination in science education.

## *The Contemporary View*

The various studies of and theories about creativity generated in recent years have not been in universal agreement about the nature of creativity, and have differed in many details, for example the extent to which creativity can be measured or the relative importance of cognitive versus personality factors. Nonetheless there do seem to be a number of salient common features among these views, and shared beliefs about the nature of creativity.

1) One common belief is that creativity is intimately connected with *originality* understood in terms of the generation of novelty. Creativity is seen to involve that which is new, divergent, and disconnected with the usual, the ordinary, the accepted. Thus it is thought to involve a radical break with the past and with existing traditions, and a fundamental change in conceptual frameworks.

2) Ths belief regarding the discontinuity involved in creativity is the basis of another of the common assumptions, that the *value* of creative products cannot be objectively determined. If creativity is characterized by a radical break with past traditions and their accompanying conceptual schemes, then it appears that there are no standards according to which creative works can be assessed, and that their evaluation is entirely subjective.

3) This problem of the evaluation of products leads, according to this line of reasoning, to the conclusion that it cannot be the production of products which is central to creativity. Thus we have another basic belief of the contemporary view, that creativity is not characterized essentially by the production of a valuable *product*, but rather by a specific mode of thinking or *process*. This creative process is identified most readily by how it differs from ordinary thinking. Ordinary thinking, according to this view, is characterized by logic, habit, rigidity, strict judgment, and the adherence to previously established rules and patterns. Creative thinking, on the other hand, is marked by leaps of imagination, irrational processes, rule-breaking, the suspension of judgment, and the spontaneous generation of ideas. It is also assumed that some individuals will be better able to engage in this process than others because of their cognitive and personality traits, and so creativity is viewed primarily as a characteristic of *persons*, irrespective of specific achievements.

4) Because this creative process is considered to be, of necessity, free and unconstrained, involving as it does the breaking of rules and established patterns, the *rules*, *skills*, and *knowledge* of specific disciplines are thought to be constraining, locking one into the prevailing conceptual framework.

5) Creativity is, then, thought to involve *something more* than skill, an imaginative element which is transcendent, irreducible, and essentially inexplicable.

This way of viewing creativity has definite implications for education and has significantly affected educational practice. It has resulted in a move away from an emphasis on excellence in specific disciplinary areas and toward an emphasis on novelty, on freedom from constraints, on thinking considered independently of any particular subject, and on personality development.

## *Problems with the Contemporary View*

A detailed examination of this view of the nature of creativity reveals, however, that it is conceptually confused, largely incoherent, and substantively false. The aim of this work is to demonstrate these problems and in the process, to elucidate a way of looking at creativity which might help to clarify some of the conceptual confusions surrounding the topic, and to provide a more adequate basis for educational theory and practice.

Each of the following chapters takes a critical look at one of the aspects of the contemporary view outlined previously. The first chapter explores the connection between originality and creativity. It challenges the notion that creative works display a radical discontinuity with previous products and argues that the originality of creative products can only be understood with reference to the traditions out of which they develop. Furthermore, the centrality of novelty for creativity is seriously questioned, and it is argued that it is really significance rather than novelty which is the primary determinant of creativity.

This notion of significance is explored further in the second chapter, which deals with the seemingly problematic nature of the evaluation of creative works. Here the argument is made that there are objective criteria for the evaluation of creative products, and that these are provided, to a considerable extent, by the existing traditions out of which the works develop. It is the overall aims of a discipline, its overarching problems and guiding methodology, and its general criteria for assessment which are the basis for determining the significance of creative products, even those which depart from some aspect of the tradition as it exists.

The third chapter, which contains the core of our argument, confronts the notion that creativity cannot be viewed in terms of the production of valuable products, but must be seen, rather as a characteristic of persons who engage in a specific process of

Introduction 5

thought. The idea that there is a distinctive creative process or mode of thinking, different from ordinary, logical thinking is shown to be mistaken, as is the derivative notion of a distinctive creative personality. Consequently, the only coherent way in which to view creativity is in terms of the production of valuable products.

The characterization of creativity as essentially rule-breaking is the focus of chapter four. The argument that rules are constraining and inhibiting to creativity is refuted, and a case is made for the central importance of knowledge, rules, skills, and methods of specific disciplines for creativity.

The final chapter deals with the claim that there is an imaginative element involved in creativity which transcends rules and skills, an element which renders creativity essentially inexplicable. It is shown in this chapter that imagination and skill are intimately connected and that an understanding of this connection can go a long way toward explaining aspects of creativity which may at first appear to defy explanation.

The upshot of this investigation is that the contemporary view of creativity is radically defective, based on unfounded claims, dubious interpretations of research, and considerable conceptual confusion. Moreover, the pedagogical practice which this view has engendered undermines the skills and knowledge which make creativity possible. The view of creativity which is developed in the pages that follow is offered as an alternative conception, one which avoids the pitfalls of the contemporary view and which promotes the development of the traditions of knowledge and culture which are the arenas of human creative achievement.

**NOTES**

1. Plato *Ion* 543b.
2. E. Paul Torrance, "Scientific Views of Creativity and Factors Affecting its Growth," *Daedalus, Journal of the American Academy of Arts and Sciences* 94 (Summer 1965): 663.
3. J.P. Guilford, "Creativity," *American Psychologist* 5 (1950): 444-54.
4. Guilford, "Creativity;" E. Paul Torrance, *Torrance Tests of Creative Thinking* (Princeton: Personnel Press, 1966); F. Barron, *Creativity and Psychological Heath* (Princeton: Van Nostrand, 1963); D.W. MacKinnon, "The Personality Correlates of Creativity: A Study of American Architects," in G.S. Nielson, ed., *Proceedings of the Fourteenth Congress on Applied Psychology* 2 (Copenhagen: Munksgaard, 1962), pp. 11-39.

5. See, for example, E. Paul Torrance, *Education and the Creative Potential* (Minneapolis: The University of Minnesota Press, 1963); *Rewarding Creative Behaviour* (Englewood Cliffs: Prentice Hall, 1965); Sidney Parnes, and A. Meadow, "Development of Individual Creative Talent," in C.W. Taylor and F. Barron, eds., *Scientific Creativity: Its Recognition and Development* (New York: Wiley, 1963), pp. 311-320; Edward De Bono, *Lateral Thinking* (London: Ward Lock Educational, 1970).

# Chapter I

# ORIGINALITY

THE IMPORTANCE of the notion of creativity in contemporary society and the consequent impetus toward fostering originality are often manifested in terms of an emphasis on novelty and divergence. This is particulary true in the arts where unique works that deviate from existing norms are the vogue and where education is frequently geared toward individual expression and the production of unusual responses. And even in the field of science, a domain traditionally oriented to tradition, there has been a recent focus on innovation and radical change in thinking about scientific discoveries and on divergence and imagination in science pedagogy.

These views and practices take as a point of departure the assumption that creative works are not simply continuations and extensions of the relevant tradition, be it artistic or scientific, but rather exhibit a radical break with previous products and a discontinuity with these traditions. This point is made by Hausman when he states:

> First of all, it should be evident that a created object exhibits a complex structure that is new and is unprecedented and unpredicted. It appears to be unaccounted for by its antecedents and available knowledge, and it is thus disconnected with its past. In this sense, it occurs in the midst of discontinuity.[1]

And Kuhn's description of scientific revolutions also stresses the lack of continuity between scientific products and their antecedents:

> Scientific revolutions are here taken to be those non-cumulative developmental episodes in which an older paradigm is replaced in whole or in part by an incompatible new one.[2]

This notion that novelty is the central feature for the originality of creative works is fraught with problems, however, problems which will be investigated in the course of this chapter and the following one. This investigation will involve a detailed exploration of the concept of originality, guided by the following questions. What are the criteria for ascribing originality to a work? How central is novelty to our ascriptions of creativity? Is radical discontinuity a feature of creative works?

## *Originality, Novelty, and Continuity*

What is involved in our ascription of originality? There does seem to be a close link between the concept of originality and that of novelty. That something is original implies that it is new in some manner.

How, then, do we identify something as an innovation or judge it as original? We must recognize in it a significant difference from what has come before. Something which is new is different in some way from that which is old or past. It is different from other things out of which it has developed, or which are of a similar kind. Thus something which is new will be like its predecessors in some ways, will be part of an existing category or framework, will be connected with a tradition or discipline but will depart from the framework in other ways. The degree to which particular innovations depart from existing frameworks varies. Some creations may be new in some small way but remain, in most ways, much like other members of the same category, while others may differ quite radically. Nevertheless some type of connection to previous products does seem to be necessary for our recognition of difference and thus of novelty.

Could something not be completely new, however, in the sense of being unconnected with anything that came before? The upholders of a dominant tradition might maintain that a new creation which breaks with the tradition in a radical way does not belong to the tradition. In the visual arts, for example, the members of the prevailing school frequently reject works which depart from the canons of that school and in fact, deny their connection with the tradition as a whole. The claim would not simply be, then, that found art is not good art, but rather that it is not art at all.

Such a case is not, however, an example of novelty which is totally unconnected with previous traditions. On the contrary, the very fact that one can plausibly debate about whether a certain entity is a member of a category implies that there are very likely some connections to that category. Whether or not the connections are sufficient for that entity to be accepted as a member of that category is precisely the subject for debate. In the case of found art, for example, its detractors might claim that it is not art because it does not involve the skilful manipulation of artistic media according to the principles and rules which characterize the tradition of art as we know it. Duchamp, on the other hand, would doubtless assert that his work is an extension of the artistic enterprise, involving as it does the features of expression through the use of forms and symbols and the making of aesthetic choices related to the selection of objects and the altering of their traditional context. In such a case, debate as to whether an innovation is a member of an existing category is possible precisely because the innovation has grown out of the existing framework and has enough similarity to it to lay a plausible claim to membership. Thus the connection to what has come before, to a tradition, to a framework, to a category, does enter into our judgment of something as new.

One might wonder whether any sense can be made of the idea of an innovation being completely new in the sense of being totally unconnected to anything with which we are acquainted. Might the advent of television be a candidate? Certainly the instantaneous transmission of moving images and sound was different from anything which had been known previously. Yet the instantaneous transmission of sound was a familiar phenomenon, and the reproduction of images was known through the medium of film. Granted that the technology and the immediacy were different, nonetheless there were communication media already in existence with which television has links and in light of which it could be understood. Moreover, it was in comparison to already existing communication media that the innovative nature of television could be recognized. In a similar manner, film was connected to still photography, being a reproduction of photographic images, but added movement to these images and could be recognized as new in view of this innovation. Photography itself may be seen to be a very radical innovation, and yet the existence of images, in reflections in water, for example, and their reproduction, in the form of painting, were familiar phenomena. The connections to what already existed and was familiar are quite tenuous and limited in this case, it is true, and that is what makes this a particularly radical innovation. Innovations vary as to the degree to which they conform to and depart from existing categories, and this is what distinguishes minor from revolutionary innovations. Nonetheless, it is the connections to what is familiar that render all such innovations comprehensible.

It is, in fact, difficult to imagine what something totally unconnected to anything we know would be like. We might speculate about being visited by creatures from another galaxy who engage in a form of activity with which we are entirely unfamiliar and which is completely unrelated to our history and traditions and to human needs and desires. In such a case, we would very likely be unable to comprehend their activity or objects related to it, to understand the reasons for them, or to make judgments about them. We might say of such phenomena that they are strange or unfamiliar. We would not say that they are innovations, nor that they are original. The only possibility for our attempting to understand such phenomena might be to connect them to something familiar. Are they like our games, like our communication, like our way of obtaining nourishment? Perhaps we would incorporate them into our culture as a part of ritual or religion as some primitive cultures have done with some manifestations of our civilization like the airplane and the photograph. Yet the possibility of understanding something as new or making judgments of originality seems to be based upon some recognition of similarity as well as of difference.

It might still be argued, however, that it is difficult to explain how we can understand that element which is different. It is frequently maintained that the originality of a creative work implies that the work is not simply a repetition of what has come before, nor even a predictable logical outcome of prevailing factors, but is, in some sense, unanticipated.[3] This is thought to involve a fundamental difference in conception and thus, necessarily, a discontinuity. If this is the case, then it would seem to render the intelligibility of original works problematic.

Now it is true, as we have seen above, that a work manifesting total discontinuity with its antecedents would be unintelligible to us. We would have no context within which to understand it. Yet the creative productions of humanity certainly do not exhibit such discontinuity. There are always some elements of similarity, some continuous threads that tie them to a known context. Moreover, the innovative elements seem so striking because we tend to focus on the differences and not to notice the continuities.

## *Art*

In order to further evaluate the claim of discontinuity in innovation, it might be helpful to examine more closely the nature of the differences that can constitute originality. Radical innovation tends to be the focus for analysis of originality, and yet there is a whole range of cases to which we might attribute originality and which bear examination.

Let us examine, first, originality in the arts, beginning with a fairly simple example, that of pottery. Each pot which is fashioned by a potter is unique in the sense that it bears the idiosyncracies of that individual at that moment, and thus is not exactly like any other. This is one of the reasons why we value pottery. It is not a mass produced item but bears the stamp of an individual. Nonetheless, not all pots would be considered original. Some might be thought to be quite ordinary. What would constitute an original pot? The first example of a pot with a handle or spout in a setting where pots formerly had neither of these would likely be considered original. Here there would be a difference from pots which had come before and the difference would be of practical value. It would make life easier. It would constitute an improvement according to a fairly easily recognizable criterion of value. In addition, a pot which was different in shape or design from what was previously the fashion and was particularly pleasing because of this might be considered original. A pot which was simply pleasing but not unlike other pots of that culture or period would not be considered to be original. One which departed from prevailing norms to some small degree might be considered mildly original, and one which departed radically might be considered very original. A pot which was simply deviant but not especially pleasing, however, would not attain the approbation of originality, since to ascribe originality is to do more than to indicate difference. It is to indicate a difference that is positive. The criteria operational in the instance of the pleasing pot are much less explicit and easily identifiable than are those operating in the case of the spout or handle. Nonetheless there must be some standards of merit, be they practical or aesthetic, according to which works of craft such as pots are judged as original.

Let us now turn to an examination of originality as it relates to painting. A painting is in some sense a unique creation, being a unique product of the individual in much the same way as a pot. Yet in painting there seems to be even more scope for differences than in the case of pottery. Paintings may differ as to subject matter, media, and style. But even two paintings of the same subject painted in a similar style and in the same medium will be somewhat different one from another, each bearing to some extent the unique imprint of the individual artist. Yet some paintings are unoriginal. Something more than uniqueness, then, is necessary for a painting to be original.

One possibility is that the originality consists in a new way of viewing a subject. Even a painting in a representational style is, after all, not simply an exact representation of a subject; rather, the subject is interpreted and transformed in some manner in the course of being portrayed. It is transformed into another medium, paint on canvas, and transfigured via an imaginative, affective component and in light of aesthetic considerations. The artist does not simply represent a subject, but chooses, adds, eliminates, changes, simplifies and composes. Thus a particular painting will exemplify a particular way of seeing the subject, a particular point of view. This point of view may be new and unexpected, capturing an aspect of the subject previously unnoticed or unexplored.

In addition to the treatment of subject matter, a painting may exhibit freshness in the choice of subject matter or ideas expressed, or in the manner in which a technique is used or extended, while still remaining faithful to an accepted framework. Poussin's creation of structure and spatial sculpture based on themes and figures borrowed from antiquity would exemplify this type of originality. We may say of a painting that it is unoriginal, and here we would imply that, despite any individual idiosyncracies, it presents a point of view which is cliché and expected and does so in a quite conventional manner.

Some works of art may differ in a very fundamental way from their contemporaries. They may break radically from the accepted style of the prevailing school, creating a new style or genre, and innovating in a revolutionary way. In such cases, differences and novelty are readily apparent. The Impressionists or Picasso would be good examples of innovative artists who broke with traditional approaches and developed new styles. Moreover Picasso upset traditional assumptions about the nature of painting itself in deliberately contravening rules of representational art. The innovations in such cases would be readily acknowledged, at least in retrospect, as original.

It is such cases as these, when there is a radical break with existing frameworks, that originality seems most striking, and it is such cases that frequently serve as the model for discussions of originality. Yet, as we have seen, there is in actuality a whole range of cases to which originality can be and is attributed, and in some of these, at least, there seems to be no difficulty in understanding the origin or seeing the continuity in conception. A pot exhibiting a somewhat novel design or shape is an unproblematic case in point. What, then, is the justification for suddenly, at some point in the continuum of differences that constitute originality, seeing the products as discontinuous?

One reason might relate to the idea that original products must be unanticipated and unpredictable.[4] The fact that one may not be able to predict a specific creation in advance does not, however, imply that one cannot explain it *post facto* in the light of what one knows of the antecedent factors and conditions. It is, in fact, precisely in terms of these factors and conditions that the innovation is comprehensible. The novel element arises in the context of an enterprise that has a history and is part of a tradition; and the tradition has a direction, goals, and meaning in light of which the innovation can be understood.

This can be seen with respect to the examples of Picasso and the Impressionists cited previously. In neither case is gratuitous novelty what is involved. The innovations in the case of works which we would call original are to an end — in order to explore a virgin area, solve a problem, or create a certain effect. Picasso's juxtapositions and reorganizations of the human figure were not a product of mere whim but were manifestations of the attempt to grapple with the problems inherent in the simultaneous portrayal of many perspectives. Similarly, the departures from tradition of the Impressionists involved, among other things, experiments in portraying the effects of light in nature. Thus continuity with the history of the art seems to be evident even in cases of quite radical originality.

Let us extend this analysis to an examination of originality in some other artistic fields, beginning with literature. As is the case for the visual arts, there is, in literature, an entire range of cases which might be considered original, extending from revolutionary innovations to modest departures. Some works of literature depart from existing traditions in a fundamental way and are radically innovative. This may involve breaking with the rules of form of an existing genre, or even creating an entirely new genre. Absurdist plays would exemplify the first type of innovation, involving the rejection of some conventional ideas about the nature of drama, such as logical plot and character development. Much modern poetry, (such as that of e.e. Cummings) with its rejection of standard poetic form and punctuation, would be another example. An example of the creation of a new genre would be the stream of consciousness novel as with James Joyce. A literary work might also innovate by treating a new subject matter, one which was previously considered to be outside the proper purview of literature. Ibsen's *Ghosts*, in dealing with the previously taboo subject of venereal disease, would be innovative for this reason. Even in these cases of radical literary innovation, however, the novelty exhibited is not random, but is in response to the problems of technique and of expression of the relevant literary tradition.

Most works of literature are not so radically innovative, however, and do adhere to the prevailing framework to a great extent. But even here the possibility of originality exists, in much the way that it does in the case of painting. The perspective on or treatment of a subject matter may be fresh, and this is a function of the mode of expression. What distinguishes literature from other types of writing is that the way something is said constitutes a part of what is said. Thus the manner in which an old subject is treated can provide fresh insights. A particular description or turn of phrase, a particular metaphor or simile, may evoke a mood or elicit an emotion or thought or response which is quite unexpected or new. An author may furnish new insights through extending an existing form, for example Henry James and his extension of narrative technique, thereby affording the reader a new perspective.

What would constitute lack of originality in literature? Here 'Harlequin Romances' might come to mind. They would be considered unoriginal because they are formula novels involving hackneyed subject matter treated in an entirely predictable manner. Indeed, the epithet 'formula' implies just this sort of unoriginal repetition of a framework or structure with only minor changes in specific details and expressed in language that does not convey a fresh insight into the conventional subject matter.

The originality examined to this point relates both to formal innovation and to new insights generated by the manner in which the subject is expressed in existing forms. Let us see how originality might be manifested in an art in which there is not an external subject matter in the same way that there can be in literature or in the visual arts, namely music. The most striking examples of musical compositions which would be deemed original would be those which depart from existing forms and are an embodiment of a new form, for example the works of Stravinsky.

It is less clear what would constitute originality in the case of works which conform to an existing framework or genre, however. In the realm of music, works do not really afford new insights by the way an external subject matter is represented. Rather, what is important here is the form itself, and its effects. Wherein, then, might lie the originality in a work in which the form does not depart radically from existing forms? Perhaps it might relate to what is done with the form, how it is used and what is achieved within its constraints. The originality of some of Bach's compositions, for example, might be seen to consist in their exploitation of Baroque form to the full, achieving what was previously not thought possible within the fugue form. *The Art of Fugue*, with its demonstration of all types of fugal writing, and *A Musical Offering*, with extensive exploration of a single subject, both exemplify this kind of accomplishment. Such achievement had to have been based on extraordinary skill and such a high degree of mastery on the part of the composer that he was able to go beyond what had previously been done within that form. Similarly, the greatness of many of the works of Mozart is based, not on the innovativeness of the form, but rather on its perfection, based on absolute mastery. This point can be further exemplified by the following observation about Vivaldi, Rameau, Bach, and Handel:

> All were aware of the new currents in musical thought, though none was a deliberate revolutionary in his own music. All worked within the established forms and styles of the late Baroque, and their originality consisted chiefly in doing things in a uniquely excellent way.[5]

What is most important with reference to at least some of the works of the above is not the formal novelty of the works, but rather the consummate skill which is manifested in their execution. Thus originality of form is not always what we are primarily interested in with regard to a piece of music nor the prime criterion for its evaluation. Some composers have achieved outstanding results within the constraints of existing forms, have gone beyond what had previously been achieved within those forms, and herein lies their originality.

Some arts such as music and drama, are more complex since they involve the initial creation of the seminal work, the script or score and also its performance. In the case of drama, the director generally begins the process with a pre-détermined and fixed script, and so there are constraints upon the creating from the outset. Nonetheless, there is considerable leeway in how the script is brought to life on stage, and this provides possibilities for originality and freshness. The most radical sort of innovation would be a change in production which transforms the way the art is practised thereafter. The growing illusionism of nineteenth century theatrical production, with the introduction of local colour in costuming, the box set with realistic detail, hidden scene changes, and advances in stage lighting would constitute a change of this magnitude.

Even where there is no extreme alteration in the conventions of the contemporary theatre, however, there may still be originality in terms of the specific interpretation of the play manifested in the production. A script is the basis for a theatrical production, but within the confines of what is actually presented in the script, there is vast scope for interpretation. The interpretation of the characters, both overall and at any particular moment, and the decision as to the meaning of the play, as well as the means to achieve these, are left to the judgment of the director. A particular production may, then, differ radically in interpretation from past productions of the same play, and might be considered quite original because of this. This would only be the case, however, if the interpretation were considered valid and supportable by the text, and if it provided fresh insights into the play. The first production of *Hamlet* in modern dress might be an example of this kind of originality, as might a recent television production of *Anthony and Cleopatra* which portrayed the lovers as senescent and doting rather than as noble and beautiful.

Even in productions in which the way in which a play is treated is not a radical departure from conventional approaches, there will still be a specific interpretation guiding what transpires, which is, in some respects, unique. There may be a particular portrayal, a particular interaction, a particular moment which conveys a fresh perception. The possibility for this type of diversity is particularly strong in drama because of the variety of factors involved in the mounting of a theatrical production. Productions will vary not only because of the director's overall interpretation, but also because of the unique performances of the individual actors and the particular circumstances of their interaction with the audience on each occasion.

This idea of interpretation comes into play, as well, in the sphere of musical performance. Although the content and manner of musical performance is largely prescribed in the score, there is nonetheless scope for variety in the execution. A performance which gives a fresh interpretation to a piece of music, which explores new and unexpected possibilities in a work would be deemed original. Nonetheless, what is of primary interest with reference to the performance of a musical work is not so much how new the interpretation is, but rather, how well it is executed. An original interpretation may make this performance special, but originality is not the only, nor even the main criterion of merit.

In the field of dance, there are various possibilities for originality which parallel to a degree those in the other arts. There can be radical innovations in form, involving breaking away from traditional forms and creating new ones, for example the creation of modern dance. There can be innovative choreography within an existing form, and there is also the possibility for a particularly fresh interpretation of an existing work.

There do seem to be differences between the various art forms as to the scope there is for divergence within the form. Two pots may be almost identical in a way in which two dramatic performances will not be. What is more, there seem to be more possibilities for radically different interpretations in dramatic productions than in musical performance. Such differences relate to the constraints which are operating with respect to the various arts, which may either restrict the possibilities, or open them up. A potter, for example, is constrained by the properties of the clay and by the properties of pots, and there is only a certain degree to which the potter can deviate and still be making a pot. It would be difficult to come up with a radically new pot. A performance of traditional music is defined quite strictly by the score, although there is certainly some leeway for interpretation, both in terms of elements which the composer has left open by convention, and those which cannot be strictly specified in the notation (for example the precise degree of loudness).[6] The performance is also limited by the properties of the musical instrument which will vary to some extent, but not radically. In a dramatic production, however, there is considerable leeway because of the variety of factors involved. The outcome will depend on the script, which cannot delineate the action very strictly, the individual differences of the actors, including their physical presence, voice, manner of movement and acting style, and the particular style of the director as well as the explicit interpretation. Thus the possibility for widely differing productions, as well as of quite radically new approaches, seems to be very great. Drama is, however, generally based on a text of some sort, whereas dance is limited only by the possibilities of choreography. This constitutes a respect in which dance presents greater possibilities for innovation.

What, then, can be concluded thus far from our examination of the manner in which the notion of originality is applied in the arts? First, it seems clear that originality is not a simple attribute which a work of art either exhibits or fails to exhibit. Rather, cases of originality lie on a continuum, ranging from minor variations within constraints to major changes which alter some aspects of the constraints themselves. In all these cases, however, connections with past products and with the history of the tradition are evident. Moreover, although some degree of novelty is connected with ascriptions of originality, it is not random or gratuitous novelty. Originality is connected with differences that make a difference, that meet a need, solve a problem, contribute to the development of the art. Indeed, it appears that it might be significance in terms of this ability to solve a problem which is of primary concern in our assessment of the creativity of works of art and not novelty.

## *Science and Technology*

Science is the other major realm of human endeavour in which creativity is seen to occur, and here too, as for art, the radical novelty of created products has, of late, been emphasized. Revolutionary scientific discovery is considered to be the locus of originality in science, and such revolutionary developments are viewed, by some, as discontinuous with previously accepted theories in the area.

Thomas Kuhn is perhaps the leading theorist to make the case for discontinuity in theory change in science.[7] Kuhn draws a sharp distinction between revolutionary science and normal science. Normal science describes ordinary scientific practice, that activity which takes place according to a fixed paradigm or framework which serves as a guide to research, specifying the problems to be undertaken and the procedures, rules and standards to be used in investigating these problems. Such normal scientific activity is highly rule-bound, uncritical of the assumptions of the paradigm, and essentially unoriginal.

Revolutionary science, on the other hand, is characterized by a radical departure from the prevailing paradigm. It involves the overthrow of the presuppositions underlying the old paradigm, and the establishment of a radically new framework. This new framework or paradigm is not simply a logical outcome or continuation of the previous one, but involves a radically new way of viewing phenomena and is, thus, incommensurable with the old paradigm. The postulation and acceptance of the heliocentric view of planetary organization would be an example of this kind of revolutionary science, upsetting the presupposition that centrality and fixity were necessary properties of the earth, and establishing a whole new framework for astronomical observations and theory. Likewise, the theory of relativity, involving as it did a radical change in our concept of time, would also exemplify revolutionary science.

For Kuhn, all scientific practice is of one of these two distinct kinds. It is either normal science, in which the implications of a paradigm are worked out in a systematic way and puzzles are solved according to established methods, or it is revolutionary science, in which old paradigms are overthrown and radically novel theories are invented. Originality is not an important feature of the former type of scientific research. It is the essence of the latter.

This radical distinction between revolutionary science and normal science cannot hold up under scrutiny, however. Numerous historians and philosophers of science have demonstrated that even scientific discoveries of an apparently revolutionary kind have their roots in the problems and the paradigms of previous theories, that there are continuities between successive theories, and that scientific development is more gradual than the Kuhnian model suggests. Hattiangadi, for example, outlines Newton's development of the law of gravitation in terms of entirely logical and cogent physical and mathematical arguments based upon reflection on theories of the time.[8] Brown emphasizes the continuity between successive theories and makes the following comment with respect to Einstein's 'revolutionary' discoveries:

> Beginning from an existing theory, i.e. an answer to a question, Einstein gives reasons why this answer is inadequate and proposes a new solution, one which may be quite different from the one he rejects but which nonetheless takes its departure from some of the ideas of the rejected hypothesis. ... Einstein consciously built his new theory on a foundation provided by the classical physics he was overturning.[9]

And Miller's historical account of the seminal developments in early twentieth century physics demonstrates clearly that the transformations of concepts involved in these discoveries were gradual. Miller vividly describes "the struggles that constitute some of the fine structure in the transition between the old and new quantum theories"[10] and he summarizes the implications for the notion of scientific revolutions as follows:

> The notion of scientific revolutions describes only the gross structure of scientific change. In the fine structure, where change is gradual, resides the fascinating problem of the nature of creative scientific thinking.[11]

It appears, then, that in the realm of science as in the realm of art, a radical dichotomy between revolutionary and non-revolutionary achievement is misleading and inaccurate. All scientific activity essentially involves working out the problems posed by the history of the tradition, and so science does not seem to be characterized by two radically different kinds of practice, one highly original and the other not. Rather, scientific products lie on a continuum ranging from mildly to highly original, similar to works of art.

The discussion to this point has centred on scientific discovery that is concerned with the postulation of new theories. Theories are not, however, the only types of products of scientific inquiry. Inquiry sometimes results in the discovery of new entities, and there is scope for the attribution of originality in such cases, as well. Theoretical innovation definitely has the potential for originality. A new theory, if accepted, provides the possibility for rethinking a discipline or an aspect of a discipline. It makes fundamental changes in the way phenomena are viewed and thus opens up the possibility for new directions in research. The case is somewhat different with respect to the discovery of a new entity. Some such discoveries would involve simply adding a new piece of information to an existing corpus, the discovery of a new moon around Jupiter, for example. This would be an interesting discovery, but not revolutionary and not really original. Some other discoveries, such as the discovery of a new type of entity, would necessitate a change in some of our basic assumptions in the area, and these would involve originality, at least in the initial conception. In the case of the discovery of the black hole, for example, the initial conception that such a celestial body, which behaved quite differently from any with which we were acquainted, must exist was a highly original idea. The idea was subsequently borne out by observations, completing the process of discovery. Similarly, the discovery of a new vaccine would be a valuable contribution, but with its use limited to the specific disease for which it was designed. The initial idea of vaccination, on the other hand, had far-reaching implications and provided an entirely new approach to dealing with certain types of diseases.

The question might arise at this point as to the importance of originality in the area of scientific investigation, and, although this will be treated fully in the next chapter, let us look briefly at the question here. How important is it that a discovery be original? If a cure were discovered for cancer which was not radically different in form from present treatments, a new drug for example, it would nonetheless be valued highly. Its originality or lack thereof would be irrelevant. What would matter would be its efficacy. The reason that originality is usually deemed important, however, seems to relate to the possibilities engendered by a new approach to a problem. An original cure for cancer might have implications for the treatment of disease as a whole. Original works often do open up new areas for exploration, and new possibilities are frequently provided by innovations.

The field of invention is one which bears examination in any discussion of originality since there is a notion of novelty and originality implicit in the very idea of invention. Here too, however, originality does not appear to be an all or nothing affair. There is, again, a range of cases which might be considered to exhibit originality. An inventor is usually setting out to solve a new problem or to deal with an old problem in a new way, and what is created may be quite radically new and original. The light bulb would be an invention of this type, solving the problem of lighting in a new and effective way. An invention may, however, simply consist in an improvement to something already existing, where the conception of the initial invention is taken over, but the invention itself is altered. The use of a tungsten filament in a light bulb was an improvement which made the light bulb practical, but was not, in itself, a radical innovation. Both of these kinds of invention exhibit some originality, although there is a difference in degree. There are new elements in the derivative invention, but these exist within the context of the original object, and it is to this primary invention that we would attribute most originality. In all cases of invention, however, it is effectiveness in solving a problem or meeting a need which gains the product the ascription of originality. Products which are merely deviant would not be considered original.

This connection to problem-solving ability gives rise to the question of the relationship between technology and invention. Do innovative ideas create the problems which generate a technology to carry them out, or do inventions arise from advances in technology in isolation from any particular problems? In point of fact, both seem to be the case, along with numerous cases which lie somewhere in between. Some examples of the spectrum of possibilities can be found in the space programme. The initial efforts in space were based on exciting new ideas, and a new technology arose in response to the problem of attempting to execute these ideas and make space flight a reality. The technology involved in the space shuttle, however, was not fundamentally new, but an extension of already existing technology, in order to carry out what was an innovative idea—a reusable space craft. Some of the actual technology developed in the space programme, however, found application in other spheres and gave rise to new products. These new products met needs and solved problems outside the space programme. In this case, the technology gave rise to the new idea; what one was capable of doing was the basis for what was done.

In such cases of innovation where there is evident both an idea and its execution, one might wonder where, precisely, the originality lies. The realm of science fiction can provide a range of examples. In some types of science fiction works, new ideas are generated in great profusion, but these ideas are not limited by scientific reality. They are marked by unbounded imagination and flights of fantasy and can be utterly fascinating and provocative. They are usually not executable, however, even potentially, since they contravene existing laws of science, and so they are not a source for solving scientific or practical problems. The idea of a time machine is intriguing, but does not further our scientific knowledge nor provide the basis for investigation nor innovation. This type of science fiction writing may possibly be original from a literary point of view, depending upon how it is written, but remains, from a scientific point of view, merely interesting. Science fiction featuring speculative science, on the other hand, involves new ideas which are plausible extensions of known scientific theories. An idea of this type may truly be original, as it may be innovative and different, and provide the basis for research and technological advance. It is a new idea which, as well as being imaginative, also has the possibility of being realized. It is with actual achievement that the idea and the technology merge to create an original product. It is the interaction of skill and imagination that gives rise to the creation, and the nature of this interaction seems to vary from case to case.

## *Mathematics*

Another area which is often seen to involve creativity and originality is that of mathematics. In this domain, as in the others examined thus far, it is initially tempting to accept the notion of a radical difference between routine, unoriginal work within the accepted framework and creative, original boundary-breaking. But this type of distinction presents an overly simplistic and inaccurate picture of practice in this domain, as well. It is true that in working on problems within a specified system of mathematics, one may apply established methods to arrive at a solution, and there may be a correct solution or solutions to the problem. This does not imply, however, that the solving of mathematical problems at this level is a totally mechanical process. There is often considerable choice as to how to approach the problem, and as to which specific procedures to use at certain points, and there is a considerable degree of understanding required in order to be able to characterize the problem and make these choices. Thus there is scope, even within specified systems, for coming up with a new method of solution to a problem. And such a new method for solution might gain significance in the discipline if it satisfies criteria of mathematical elegance to a greater extent than previous methods or displays connections previously unnoticed.

Some of the work of mathematicians consists in attempting to characterize new classes of problems, provided either by science or by mathematics itself, and to explore the implications of these, and such work results in the formulation of new proofs or theorems, or entirely new systems. One example of this type of mathematical innovation would be the invention of analytic geometry. This was a very significant innovation, and yet what was involved was essentially an extension of existing mathematics in the form of a synthesis of algebra and geometry. It involved a fundamentally new perspective, but there was no contradiction of existing mathematical concepts. In addition, innovative developments in mathematics may sometimes involve a change in one of the presuppositions of the prevailing system. The development of non-Euclidian geometries, for example, depended upon the realization that one could consistently change the axiom of Euclidian geometry that parallel lines do not meet, a change which was quite revolutionary. This sort of mathematical activity, when one is working at the edge of knowledge, can produce innovations which fundamentally change the discipline and open up a new area of exploration and a new set of problems to be solved. Nonetheless, much of the previous framework remains intact even in such cases of radical innovation.

The field of logic exhibits an array of cases of originality similar to that evident in mathematics. Even when dealing with problems within a specified framework where there is a correct solution or set of solutions to a problem, one might exhibit originality in coming up with a new method in order to arrive at it. A considerable degree of originality would be involved in the establishment of a new system which extends or even supersedes the prevailing one, the development of symbolic logic, for example. Another sort of innovation which would be deemed original in this domain would be a new idea, a theorem for example, developed when the rules of the prevailing system are tested to their limit, and one or some must give way. Gödel's theorem would exemplify such an innovation, showing that any axiomatic system, of the type which *Principia Mathematica* exemplifies, is necessarily incomplete since there will always be true statements in it which are unprovable.

## *Problem-Solving and Originality in Everyday Life*

Problem-solving is an activity which is not limited to science or mathematics, however, but pervades all facets of our lives. Indeed, much of the focus of attempts to foster creativity seems to be toward encouraging people to deal with a greater degree of originality with everyday problems. Thus it seems important to examine what the possibilities are for originality with regard to dealing with everyday, real-world problems.

De Bono uses a certain type of problem to exemplify problems which require creativity and originality in their solution. These are problems which have a set solution which is difficult to arrive at by straight deductive reasoning, and De Bono claims that the difficulty people tend to experience in solving such problems typifies the rigidity and lack of originality they display with respect to everyday problems.[12] How applicable is the notion of originality in this context, however? There is a right answer to each of these sorts of problems, a previously established and accepted solution. The problem may even have been set up subsequent to the idea of a type of solution. Thus the modes of solution are not new, and there cannot be originality in a situation where the problem-solving activity exhibits no novelty. The initial devising or solving of such problems may have involved some originality, and coming up with a new, unanticipated solution may, as well, but arriving at an already established solution through already established means does not seem to qualify. The thrust of De Bono's argument might be that the thinking process required to arrive at such solutions is not the normal deductive mode, but is unusual, and that herein lies the originality. It may be that the type of thinking involved in solving such problems is not strictly deductive, but involves going beyond the given information, but calling such thinking original seems to imply a newness which is not evident. De Bono advocates procedures to facilitate such thinking, and although they may not be those of deductive reasoning, they are nonetheless procedures to arrive, in these examples, at set solutions. It is at this point an open question whether such methods might help one to come up with original creations, but the act of solving one of De Bono's trick closed problems does not, itself, exhibit originality.

There is one very fundamental difference between the type of problem De Bono outlines and the types of problems one confronts in everyday life. While the former are problems which have a right answer, the latter are open-ended problems, problems for which there is not one correct solution, nor is the form of solution nor the procedure for arriving at it specifiable in advance. There may even be disagreement, when a potential solution is proffered, as to its efficacy. There may, however, be standard approaches for dealing with such problems, and a departure from these, and one that works, might constitute originality in this type of problem-solving. The difficulty in ascribing originality in this area concerns the fact that there are not always clear criteria for establishing when a solution has been achieved. Let us examine some examples of open-ended problems to illustrate these points. An economic problem such as inflation exemplifies a problem for which there is no agreed upon solution, and there is, indeed, much controversy as to the best approach for attempting a remedy. The criterion for deciding when the problem is solved may seem clear-cut, namely a decline in the inflation rate, but even here there are other factors to be taken into consideration, such as the side effects of the strategy undertaken, which may still leave room for disagreement as to whether a proffered solution is adequate. Another example of an open-ended problem might be the social inequalities resulting from industrialization. Here there are a wide variety of possibilities for attempting a solution, ranging from attempting to implement existing strategies, to devising new approaches to deal with the new problems within the context of the existing system, to proposing an entirely new socio-economic system. Such approaches vary in their radicalness, from totally conventional, to making adjustments and adaptations within a system but still accepting the basic framework and premises of that system, to major revolutionary change involving the overthrow of the system. Moreover, there are no clear criteria for determining an adequate solution. There would not, for example, be agreement between an arch conservative and a socialist as to the best approach! Thus, with reference to problem-solving dealing with open-ended problems, various degrees of novelty are possible, but the assessment of value which seems to be connected with our notion of originality, is difficult to determine.

Problem-solving is not limited to the kind of broad spectrum problems just outlined, however, but takes place, as well, in our daily lives. One may wonder, then, whether the notion of originality has any applicability in this sphere. Is it possible to display originality in solving everyday problems? One way in which everyday problem-solving is sometimes considered to exhibit originality is in terms of an individual coming up with a solution which that individual had never considered before, and thus is new to him or her. Now the ascription of originality implies, as we have seen, a comparison with other products and a reference to specific contexts. Something is original, partly, as least, by virtue of its place in the specific discipline or context. If there is a reference to the existing 'state of the art' implied in our use of the term 'originality', then the fact that a discovery is new to the individual is not relevant to the ascription of originality. What is of concern is whether or not it is new to or effects changes in the context. Now we do sometimes use the term 'originality' in everyday situations. We may say that a person has come up with an original solution to a practical problem, an original gift idea, or an original recipe. In these situations, it is not the case that these 'discoveries' or 'creations' have never been thought of before. Rather, they are new and valuable within a specific but somewhat limited context. The original gift idea may be new within the context of a certain group of people and their gift-giving traditions, but that is the extent of its scope.

Another problem with the application of the concept of originality is to what extent it is applicable with reference to the work of children. Would it be considered original if, for example, a child were to discover something which was new to her, a law of physics, perhaps? This would depend upon the precise circumstances. If a child were to discover something which was really new to the discipline as a whole, she would be considered a genius, and her prodigious feat would certainly be deemed highly original. If, on the other hand, what was discovered were based on a set of circumstances designed specifically in order to lead to that discovery (discovery learning), then the child might be considered quick or clever, but originality does not seem to enter here. What would we say in a case where a child is not given complete information or carefully structured learning situation, but makes some sort of leap in order to make a discovery on his own? We might say that he thinks independently, that he has a real insight into or deep understanding of the discipline. We might, further, say that there is a strong likelihood that he will make original discoveries in the future. Nonetheless, the discovery which he is making in this context is not new. That it is new to him means that he is learning. That he discovered it with minimal information means that he is thinking well. But the discovery itself is not original. This is meant in no way to demean the achievement. Learning in this manner may well be extremely valuable. The point is simply that the ascription of originality is not appropriate.

## 28  Achieving Extraordinary Ends

Is there any sense in which children's art could be considered original? Some highly esteemed artists such as Mozart and Picasso were child prodigies who, even at an early age, produced works which were masterful and significant, and such works certainly display originality. The more common case, however, is that of a child producing a piece which is merely unusual as compared with the work of adults or of other children. The difference in the former case might be the result either of lack of the knowledge and technique by which the adult's work is informed or of chance. The lack of technique may produce a work which is unusual because of its naivety. This may be quite charming but it is not new and significant to the whole artistic tradition, and thus is not really original in this context. A child's work which is different from what other children of that age and culture normally produce but not significant in the field might be deemed original, but it is only within this limited context of children in similar situations that such an ascription applies. If produced by chance, such works lack an additional element which seems to be necessary for originality, the element of informed intention on the part of the creator.

Our attribution of originality presupposes a creator who takes an active part in creating. Thus something produced purely randomly would not qualify. Of a painting produced by a monkey, one might say that it was different, perhaps novel, and even in some circumstances pleasing. One would not likely say that it was original.

What is the nature of the intention involved in creating? Jerome Kagan offers one possibility:

> The novelty that is a defining attribute of the creative work owes its allegiance to two forces—the availability of the diverse possibilities and, equally important, the desire to surprise. The wish to produce a unique idea sets the compass of the mind in an oblique direction and leads it to search in out-of-the way places for a course to pursue.[13]

Kagan is suggesting that, in order to create an original work, one must have the intention to surprise and to produce something new. This may well be true in some cases. An inventor may be dissatisfied with conventional approaches to a certain problem and may be setting out precisely to invent something new and better. An artist may feel that existing problems have been solved or that the art has progressed as far as it can in a certain direction, and that a radically new approach is required. Thus Picasso or Samuel Beckett may well have had the intention to create something new.

This need not always be the case, however. Frequently one's intention might be simply to solve a problem or produce a work of art, and an innovation may emerge in the process of attempting to do so. A scientist may be attempting to deal with an anomaly in an accepted theory within the framework of the theory, but be lead by difficulties in explaining the anomaly to the postulation of an entirely new theory. Postulating an entirely new theory may not have been an intention at the outset but rather a product of working on the problem. Similarly, an artist may be intending simply to paint a picture, perhaps experimenting with certain elements, and an original work may be a result of the experimentation rather than an explicit intention of the artist when he began. Mozart, for example, reflecting on his own originality, says:

> But why my productions take from my hand that particular form and style that makes them Mozartish, and different from the works of other composers, is probably owing to the same cause which renders my nose so large or so aquiline, or, in short, makes it Mozart's, and different from those of other people. For I really do not study or aim at any originality.[14]

Thus I would disagree with Kagan that the intention to surprise and to produce something novel is necessarily present in the creation of an original product. What I am maintaining, however, is that the active participation, at some level, of a conscious agent is necessary, an agent who has skills, makes choices, and is critical.

It might be argued, however, that the conscious intention of an agent is not always the motive force behind an innovation, but that chance and random elements may play a role in creation and discovery. The discovery of penicillin could be cited as an example. It does seem to be the case that random elements may enter in at various stages of a creative or discovery process. They may provide the impetus for a discovery, as in the case of penicillin, or the inspiration for a creation, as might a chance meeting provide the subject matter for a poem. They may enter in at a later stage, triggering the solution to a problem or being incorporated into a work in progress. Nonetheless, the informed participation of the creator is still necessary at some point. The scientist must take notice of the chance event and recognize its implications. He must make of it a discovery. The artist must transform any random happenings into art. Thus, although random elements may play a role in discovery, the active participation of an agent is necessary in order for us to ascribe originality to a product.

It might be claimed, however, that it is not the conscious intention of the creator which is manifested in creation, but rather her unconscious or subconscious being. Psychoanalytic theory would exemplify this point of view. If, indeed, there are unconscious elements involved in creating, then this fact may have repercussions for our claim that the active participation of the agent is a necessary condition for originality.

Freud, in his study of Leonardo da Vinci,[15] develops a possible explanation for aspects of Leonardo's personality and art in terms of certain compulsions and obsessions which stem from his childhood. He explains the intriguing smile on the faces of several of his studies, for example, as the product of an obsession with the smile of his mother and all of its evocations. Moreover, he connects the very drive to investigate and create to the repression of his sexual instincts. If we grant that unconscious factors such as those attributed by Freud to Leonardo may well operate in cases of creation (although the specific details may be in doubt), then does this detract from the picture of the creator as active intentional agent of creation? I think not. Psychoanalytic theory points out that there are reasons for one's actions in addition to those which are consciously acknowledged. This need not imply complete determinism, however. Leonardo may indeed have been obsessed with women's faces and certain facial expressions, but this does not alter the fact that he was an outstanding artist who made choices in his art relating to subject matter and execution. Other individuals may have similar repressed emotions and obsessions, but they are not necessarily artists. Leonardo, on the other hand, intended to paint, to create a work of art, to portray an image or vision, and he succeeded. That the image or vision may have been a product of infantile desires and juvenile repressions makes no difference. There is no expectation that the products of one's imagination be consciously intentional, but only that the works created from them have a component of conscious and active agency in their execution.

## *Summary*

What conclusions can be drawn from the exploration of originality which has been undertaken in the course of this chapter? First, it seems clear that the claim that created works are discontinuous with the past and involve radical breaks with tradition is totally unfounded. There are, in fact, a whole range of cases of created products which can be seen to exhibit originality, and some of these involve originality which takes place within the constraints of a tradition. And even with respect to innovations which seem to be quite revolutionary, continuities and connections with the tradition are always in evidence. Indeed, this must be the case, since such innovations can only be understood and can only gain significance in light of such traditions.

The originality involved in creativity does not reduce to arbitrary novelty. The fact that something is new is not a sufficient condition for it to be deemed creative. It may not even be a necessary condition, or at least not a primary consideration. Some of the artistic masterpieces which we value highly today are relatively non-divergent examples of the style which was prevalent at the time, the works of Rembrandt or Gainsborough for example. They are, however, outstanding examples of the style and so expertly executed that they are still highly esteemed. Similarly, the works of Bach would be considered to be highly creative, and yet they do not exhibit radical innovations of form.

The originality of creative products is valued primarily because it provides the possibility for new types of solutions to existing problems and for opening up new directions for exploration. It is, in the end, the significance of the work that counts, and this is judged against the background of existing traditions, both in terms of how the work conforms to and how it departs from these traditions. The factors which determine the significance of created works will be explored in the next chapter.

### NOTES

1. Carl Hausman, *Discourse on Novelty and Creation* (Albany: SUNY Press, 1984), p.9.
2. Thomas Kuhn, *The Structure of Scientific Revolutions* (Chicago: The University of Chicago Press, 1962), p.92.
3. Hausman, *Discourse on Novelty*.

4. Ibid.

5. Donald Jay Grout, *A History of Western Music* (New York: W.W. Norton and Company, 1980), p.402.

6. Many modern composers have deliberately introduced a greater degree of indeterminacy into their compositions, however, from the filling in of sections and the choosing of the order of execution in an otherwise fairly well specified score (eg. Stockhausen's compositions), to a complete openness of options, exemplified well by John Cage's directions in his *Variations IV*: "for any number of players, any sounds or combinations of sounds produced by any means, with or without other activities."

7. Kuhn, *Structure of Scientific Revolutions*.

8. Jagdish Hattiangadi, "The Vanishing Context of Discovery," in T. Nickles, ed., *Scientific Discovery, Logic, and Rationality* (Dordrecht: D. Reidel, 1980), pp.257-265.

9. Harold I. Brown, *Perception, Theory, and Commitment: The New Philosophy of Science* (Chicago: Precedent Publishing Inc., 1977), p.138.

10. Arthur I. Miller, *Imagery in Scientific Thought* (Boston: Birkhauser, 1984), p.301.

11. Ibid., p.312.

12. De Bono, *Lateral Thinking*. The following are examples of this type of problem:
    i) How would you arrange four trees so that each one is exactly the same distance from each of the others?
    ii) Arrange four blocks so that each block is touching one other?

13. Jerome Kagan, *Creativity and Learning* (Boston: Houghton Mifflin Company, 1967), p.viii.

14. Wolfgang Amadeus Mozart, "A Letter," Excerpt from E. Holmes, *The Life of Mozart Including his Correspondence* (Chapman and Hall, 1878), pp.211-13, in P.E. Vernon, ed., *Creativity* (Middlesex: Penguin Books, 1970), pp. 55-56.

15. Sigmund Freud, *Leonardo da Vinci: A Study in Psychosexuality*, trans. A.A. Brill (New York: Vintage Books, 1947).

# Chapter II

# VALUE

THE IDEA that creative achievement involves radical novelty and fundamental breaks with the past underlies another tenet of the common view of creativity, namely that the evaluation of creative products is problematic. If created works are discontinuous with the tradition out of which they arise, and if they break the rules and transcend the standards of the tradition, then the standards of assessment inherent in the tradition cannot provide the basis for the evaluation of these products. According to this view, then, there are no objective criteria for the evaluation of creations, and appeal must be made to subjective factors in order to explain our valuing of novel products.

This type of argument is frequently made with respect to the arts. It is argued that a radical innovation in artistic style cannot be comprehended or assessed according to the rules or standards of the previous style, because the innovation consists precisely in transcending these rules and standards. Instead, the novel work brings with it its own standards for evaluation. This is very much the Kantian notion of genius giving the rule to art.[1] Thus, for example, the cubist paintings of Picasso could not be assessed according to the canons of representational painting. Rather, they established new, unprecedented possibilities for painting which entailed entirely new criteria for evaluation.

According to this view, then, our valuing of novel works cannot be based on any comparison with past products or reference to previous standards. The alternative account which is frequently proposed is that the value of these new products is grasped in an intuitive, holistic manner. Hausman characterizes such creative products as novel forms or intelligibilities which we somehow recognize as being intrinsically valuable. He goes on to state:

> ...this kind of inherent value is attributable to a new Form by virtue of the determinate structure of the new object. It appears on condition that the specific and definite Form in question is recognized as what ought to be, not simply because it is something

determinate, but also because it is a certain kind of being which is intelligible in a definite way that ought to be.[2]

The value of novel products may be grasped in this intuitive way by a culture as a whole, as when an artistic innovation takes hold of the popular consciousness; by a group, as when an innovation is acknowledged as valuable by the experts in a field; or even by an individual. The possibility of the last of these gives rise to the notion that artistic value is radically subjective, that the only criterion for evaluation of a work is that it is valuable to an individual.

There are a number of puzzling phenomena with respect to the evaluation of works of art which seem to give support to this view that there is no objective basis for artistic value. One of these relates to the fact that the evaluation of some works changes over time. A work which is revered in one era may fall out of favour in another. Yet if there were an objective basis for assessing works, one might expect the assessment to remain constant. Another phenomenon which appears to lend support to the subjectivist position is the fact that works are not always recognized as significant during the era in which they are created, but only later. Yet the existence of objective criteria might lead one to expect immediate recognition.

This idea that the evaluation of created works is problematic has recently been extended into the realm of science. The traditional view, that the ultimate ground for assessing scientific theories lies in their accuracy in representing the world, has been seriously questioned by a number of theorists including Kuhn[3] and Feyerabend.[4] They have, moreover, suggested that there are no objective criteria according to which new scientific theories can be evaluated.[5] This view puts into the question the very rationality of the scientific enterprise, and necessitates resorting to psychological and sociological factors in order to explain the way we value scientific products.

This view that the value of created works cannot be objectively assessed rests on the assumption that such works are discontinuous with the tradition from whence they originate. This assumption has, in the course of the preceding chapter, been shown to be false. In this chapter, it will be argued that there are standards for assessing creative products. There are a variety of factors involved in our ascriptions of value, and some of these relate to existing traditions. It is the overall aims of a discipline, its overarching problems and guiding methodology, and its general criteria for assessment which are the basis for determining the significance of creative products, even those which depart from the tradition. There are, however, some differences in nature between the artistic and scientific traditions, and these give rise to differences in the grounds for the evaluation of created works in these areas.

## *Value in Art*

The value which is attributed to art in most societies is connected with its unique nature and function: it provides aesthetic experience through its mode of expression. Both Herbert Read's depiction of art as the expression of feeling in communicable form, and Suzanne Langer's characterization of art in terms of forms of feeling emphasize this expressive quality.[6] Art has a meaning or significance for people, and at least part of its significance derives from its form. It is able to have meaning and be expressive with reference to those non-discursive, affective aspects of our experience which defy formulation in ordinary language, and this is possible because the form is part of what is expressed. In poetry, for example, the meaning derives not simply from the denotation of the words, but also from what is connoted by their juxtaposition, by the emotional images evoked by their sounds, by the sensory appeal of their rhythm. In painting, the meaning goes beyond simply the subject represented to include what is evoked by the colours, the lines, the relationship of shapes, by all the aspects of form. Perhaps the ability that art has to function in this way relates to the sensuous quality of the modes of artistic expression which may be best for expressing certain aspects of experience which cannot be captured well within the rigid conceptual categories of ordinary language. This is not to say that ordinary forms of language and representation are free from emotional evocations and are purely conceptual. Even scientific language, which purports to be totally objective, cannot lay claim to this. The difference lies in the fact that, while for conceptual language such evocations are peripheral, for art they are central to its very meaning.

Once the centrality of the role of form in art is recognized, then one might proceed one step further and claim that the value of art is grounded entirely in its form. Clive Bell propounds such a view of art. According to Bell, what is significant in art is the form, and the form alone. The content of a work is irrelevant, and, in fact, a distraction from what is important, namely form. For this reason, he is highly critical of representational works in the visual arts, and views literature, which necessarily involves ideas and information, as an impure and possibly inferior art. Further implications of this view are that no knowledge from life is required in order to appreciate art, but only a sensibility to aspects of form, and that the emotions derived from art should not be the emotions of life, but only purely aesthetic emotions.[7]

This view has a certain appeal because it emphasizes the crucial role of form in art and recognizes the fact that form is what gives art significance as art. Nonetheless, one can recognize this fundamental role of form without limiting the value of art to its formal aspects.

The fundamental problem with Bell's view is that it presupposes a very definite distinction between form and content. Bell says that form alone is what is important, and seems, at times, to indicate that one could have works which were, or bordered on being, purely formal. This point of view is fundamentally flawed, however. Rather than being separate components which are simply added together to come up with a work, form and content are more like aspects of the same thing. The terms are abstractions which are helpful in discussing facets of works of art, but this need not imply that they are elements which can in reality be separated. The manner of expression in art constitutes a part of what is expressed, and it is impossible to totally isolate either form or content. If, for example, one were to ask an artist what she was trying to say in her painting or poem, her response would, in the end, have to involve indicating a work and saying, "That is what I wanted to say." Any attempt to extract a content and express it in another form is necessarily inadequate since it will no longer be the same content. Similarly, there cannot be form in isolation. A form must be a form of something, and it is difficult to imagine how one could isolate the form of a work in order to attend to it alone.

This point can be illustrated using the play *Hamlet* as an example. What is the content of *Hamlet*? Now we could talk about the content by giving a summary of the plot or by paraphrasing the dialogue, but neither of these is the content, nor can either one adequately convey what the play conveys. What exactly is the form of *Hamlet*? Again, the form can be discussed in terms of an analysis of the structure, but no analysis, no matter now detailed, is the form. The form is something which is embodied in the work. And if one were to combine such a plot and dialogue summary and structural analysis, the results would certainly not be *Hamlet*, nor anything very much like it. The terms 'form' and 'content' are useful in looking at aspects of a work of art, but the work itself is a unity. What, for example, would constitute the form of a painting? One might maintain that the form is the painting reduced to its formal elements—lines, shapes, and colours. The entire painting is composed of these elements, however, and all of them are surely necessary in order to constitute the form. Thus the form cannot really be separated from the work as a whole.

Perhaps what Bell means is that one must attend only to the formal aspects of works and not to their representational characteristics, and at times his arguments support this interpretation.[8] He claims that representational works distract both the artist and spectator from the formal aspects of a work by arousing emotions of life in a domain in which they have no place. He further contends that non-representational works allow concentration on the creation and appreciation of form. This view seems to make an arbitrary and artificial distinction between the emotions of life and aesthetic emotions, however. Art touches us because it touches our sensibility, and this is surely the same sensibility which operates in life in general. There is no reason to believe that representational content detracts from the form. Rather, it is the unique manner in which art expresses what it does that imbues it with aesthetic appeal and aesthetic value. Literature, for example, is necessarily filled with ideas and information, to use Bell's terminology, and there does not seem to be any justification for degrading its status because of its conceptual content. It does not detract from the formal aspects. Similarly, there are works of visual art in which what is represented is obviously not irrelevant and where attending to the content is essential to an appreciation of the work, *Guernica* being just one example. Works do vary as to the degree to which they are representational, but this difference is not what determines for us their value as art. Bell's view entails a rejection of a great deal of what we do consider to be art, and this rejection is based solely on his own perception of form which he can justify only with reference to his own subjective state of aesthetic emotion and aesthetic ecstasy. He seems to be stipulating a definition of art and proposing a view of aesthetic value which ignores aspects of our actual experience of art.

The value of art, then, relates to content as well as to form, and to the way the two are unified in the work. Although there may or may not be certain aspects of form which have intrinsic appeal as Bell maintains, nonetheless the nature of works of art does change, and there are numerous factors which affect what is valued at any particular time. One important factor is the state of the art itself. Whatever else art might be, it is a discipline which is passed on; it is a tradition. As such it changes and develops, it has a history, and it involves the formulation and solving of problems which are specifically artistic. The attempts to deal with certain problems may give rise to new ones, and so art changes, partially at least, through the working out of artistic problems. The way we value works of art is related, to some extent, to their place in the discipline. It is connected with the evaluation of how well they have solved the existing problems of the art, and whether they are thus good examples of their kind, or with whether they have dealt with new problems and pushed the art beyond old limits. Thus I would maintain, contrary to Bell, that our valuing of art is related to a knowledge of the tradition and of how a work fits into it or departs from it. Ernst Kris makes this point well:

> We have long come to realize that art is not produced in an empty space, that no artist is independent of predecessors and models, that he no less than the scientist and the philosopher is part of a specific tradition and works in a structured area of problems. The degree of mastery within this framework and, at least in certain periods, the freedom to modify these stringencies are presumably part of the complex scale by which achievement is being measured.[9]

Some examples from the various arts will illustrate this point. In the field of the visual arts, there are many works which we value, not because they are remarkably innovative, but because they exemplify a style so completely and demonstrate such a complete mastery of its techniques. An example would be the work of Raphael. Of him, Wight states:

> Raphael...had the ability to sum up the Renaissance. Without any apparent effort, he fulfilled the efforts of others. He broke no molds; he simply was the epoch and this is instantly understood.[10]

The valuing of some works, however, is related to their innovativeness, to how they depart from the existing tradition, as well as to how they fit into it. The works of the French Impressionists can provide a good example of this. Here the new techniques which were developed were a result of dealing with the artistic problem created by attempting to portray the effects of light, and part of our valuing of Impressionist works has to do with the recognition of this innovation. Their new techniques were not without precedent, however, being anticipated, for example, by Constable's use of broken colour and of flecks of white paint to convey light, known as Constable's snow. Nonetheless their works broke with the school of Academic painting which preceded them and expanded the horizon of painting, opening up the art to explorations in new areas.

This quality of opening up possibilities seems to be an important factor in our valuing of art. It is not enough that a work or a style be different, but this difference must play a role in the technical development of the discipline. Such an innovation has a history. Even works which break some of the rules of an existing framework will still adhere to many of them, and will, thus, have numerous connections with it. Such new works are not simply manifestations of arbitrary novelty, but have grown out of attempts to grapple with certain problems, and their value is connected with the defining of these new problems as well as with the attempts at solving them. The difference is valued because of where it occurs and why, and it will provide a new direction in which the art can develop.

This aspect of artistic value which is related to developments inherent in the discipline itself is probably most evident in music. Here the conceptual content is generally secondary to the formal aspects. Thus the solving of formal problems and the working out of the implications of formal structures is intrinsic to the development and evaluation of music. Our estimation of Bach's greatness, for example, is influenced by the extreme mastery with which he worked out the implications of the fugue form, exploiting it to a degree which was beyond anything previously imagined. Innovations in musical form can also be seen to be related to problems inherent in the musical tradition. Stravinsky's innovations in rhythm, for example, can be seen as efforts to liberate rhythm from 'the tyranny of the barline', and thus their significance can only be understood with reference to the way rhythm had evolved until that time. Even a revolutionary such as he acknowledges the importance in the development of music of tradition, which he defines as:

> a living force that animates and informs the present....Far from implying the repetition of what has been, tradition presupposes the reality of what endures. It appears as an heirloom, a heritage that one receives on condition of making it bear fruit before passing it on to one's descendants.[11]

The distinction between works which are valued because of their place within a specific framework and those which are valued as innovations is a rather artificial one, useful for the purposes of analysis, but failing to take into account the variations in the actual spectrum in art. Many revered works are combinations of the two, containing elements from the traditional discipline, but innovating in some ways, and works vary as to the degree to which they either remain traditional or innovate. Thus, both of the factors outlined previously play a role in the valuing of some works.

The evolution of form through the development and exploration of structures of the discipline is evident in literature as well. The stream of consciousness novel, perhaps best exemplified by Joyce in *Ulysses*, deals with the problem of expressing the subjective reality of an individual, and is innovative in this respect. Nonetheless, in terms of structure, it is a continuation of previous narrative forms such as that of Hardy. Similarly, the Brechtian technique of alienation in drama is a result of attempting to deal with a specifically dramatic problem, breaking down the kind of illusion which had been characteristic of naturalistic theatre. Nonetheless, the impetus for this sort of change is also related to factors which are external to the discipline of drama itself, in this case Brecht's political and social ideas which demanded an involvement in the social problems of the day. Such factors, as well as the relationship of a work to a tradition, play a role in the way works of drama and literature in general are valued, and all such factors are often interconnected in a complex web of relationships.

At this point, then, let us begin to explore some of these other factors which also affect and play a role in how we value art. One of these factors is the state of technology, both that which is directly related to the art, and that of the society in general. The vision that an artist has and the work that is produced are very much products of the technology which is available as a means of expression. Gombrich makes this point effectively:

> The artist, clearly, can render only what his tools and his medium are capable of rendering. His technique restricts his freedom of choice. The features and relationships the pencil picks out will differ from those the brush can indicate. Sitting in front of his motif, pencil in hand, the artist will, therefore, look out for those aspects which can be rendered in lines—... he will tend to see his motif in terms of lines, while, brush in hand, he sees it in terms of masses.[12]

Moreover, what is valued in art is closely related to what can be achieved—to what is possible at that stage and to what becomes possible through advances in the technology. In music, for example, the invention of the pianoforte made possible varieties of expression on keyboard which created a new basis for evaluation in this form. Similarly, the invention of oil paint changed what was possible in the art of painting, adding the ability to convey texture effectively, and so expanding the grounds for evaluation.

The field of architecture can supply many examples of this point, since it is an art which is based on technology. Changes in architectural style are closely connected with discoveries in building materials and in the technology of construction, and thus the aesthetic sensibility of a period with reference to architecture is shaped, to some extent, by the available technology. The Gothic style, for example, with its numerous arches and vaults, is not simply a manifestation of a predilection for arches at that period, but takes this form, partially, at least, because this was the technique available at that time for spans. Thus the valuing of a specific form is related, in this case, to what can be achieved technologically. The form of the modern skyscraper is likewise determined partially by available technology, involving an exploitation of the modern construction materials of steel and concrete. We do seem to value works which make use of a new technology, since such technological innovations give rise to new possibilities in form and thus to a new direction in which the art can grow.

Technological advances in areas which are only peripherally related to a specific art can also have an effect on what is valued in the art. The invention of photography, for example, no doubt had an effect on the art of painting, although the nature of this influence is by no means clear. Photography does seem to have taken over to a great extent certain areas which were previously the purview of painters, namely portraiture and landscape portrayal. One might further contend that the invention of photography freed painting from the necessity to attempt representation since this function could be performed better by photography, and this may have been a factor in the rise and acceptance of abstract art. Another example of the influence of technology would be in the area of music. The invention of the phonograph resulted in a proliferation of all types of music, popular as well as classical, and this has brought music and its evaluation into the sphere of interest of a large number of people.

Art is also shaped to a considerable extent by a combination of factors which might be called the climate of the time, factors which include the economic, political, and social conditions, as well as the state of religious, scientific, and philosophical belief. Such factors affect not only the kind of art that is produced, but also the sensibility of the time, determining what is relevant and what is acceptable. The philosophy of existentialism, for example, had a very direct bearing on literature, in the form of existentialist authors such as Camus whose philosophy was directly expressed in their writing. In addition to affecting subject matter, this philosophy also had an effect on form. Theatre of the absurd, for example, which had part of its philosophical basis in existentialism, was characterized by an abandoning of logical plot development and traditional dramatic structure. These innovative works could be understood and appreciated by audiences because existentialist thought formed part of the climate of the time. Thus the audience, or part of it, was ready to accept not only the content of these works, but also the novel formal elements—the abandoning of rules which were previously considered to be necessary to drama.

One might, further, postulate connections between scientific discoveries, with the world view entailed by them, and the state of art. One might hypothesize, for example, that the theory of relativity, at least as popularly understood, generated an overall intellectual climate in which the abandoning of rules was acceptable and, in fact, positively valued. Such a rejection of many traditional rules is certainly a characteristic of the art of this century.

The religious ideology of a period has a very real manifestation in art in terms of church architecture. The design of a church will conform to the purpose it is seen to serve and will exemplify some of the abstract ideals of the religious sentiment of the time. Wight makes this point with reference to the Gothic cathedral:

> It is really the vast windows that most truly represent the Gothic, for as the pointed arch reached for height, the great windows reached for light. For a Middle Age that rejected the earth and sought heaven, both height and light were symbols and goals.[13]

The political, economic, and social conditions of a period also play a role in determining the kind of art which is produced and valued, particularly with reference to the subject matter. Such conditions are consistently reflected in the literature of a period, its theatre, and its songs. The conditions may also shape the subject matter of works of visual art, as is evidenced by a painting such as *Guernica*. In such works, the subject matter does play a role in how they are received and viewed. The work can communicate to the audience, can touch it, because what is said is relevant and meaningful. Certainly the effect of the content is only partially the basis for the appeal of such works, however, since it is the manner in which the content is embodied which gives a work its aesthetic value. Nonetheless, in works in which there is a salient subject matter, this element cannot be ignored.

Do these ideological and environmental factors also affect the form of works of art? In some cases, they are not particularly relevant. In *Guernica*, for example, a strong political and social sentiment is the basis for the content, but the particular form of the work is determined by different sorts of factors, factors related to technical problems in the evolution of painting. Yet in some cases, a particular ideology, be it political, social, or religious, can generate principles which may find an extension and application in artistic form. The Bauhaus, for example, involved a design concept based upon a particular political ideology, namely socialism, and the design principles which were valued were those such as simplicity and functionalism which were seen to be non-bourgeois. Similarly, nationalism was a force affecting music in the nineteenth century in Europe, and this influence extended to the form and structure of the music, as Grout indicates:

> It [nationalism] underlies such externals as the choice of national subjects for operas and symphonic poems, the collecting and publishing of folk songs, and the occasional quoting of folk

tunes in compositions; but a more important consequence was the rise of new styles through fertilization of orthodox Germanic music by tonal, melodic, harmonic, rhythmic, and formal characteristics of the national idioms.[14]

We have determined, then, that the way we value art is connected to numerous factors related both to the discipline itself and to the state of the society in general. Such factors affect the manner in which art changes, and also the way we value art, since the two are closely interwoven. For the purposes of analysis, the factors have been discussed as if they were discrete and separate, but in reality it is difficult to separate them. The value of a work of art is the product of a complex interplay of such factors, which affect each other in addition to influencing art, and changes in art likely affect some of them, as well.

The preceding analysis may help to explain how we can value innovative works as well as those which conform to an existing tradition. In the latter case, the works fit into a specific framework which is characterized by rules of technique, style, and execution. With a knowledge of the tradition, we can understand the place of a specific work within it. We can compare it to others of the same genre and appreciate the skill of its execution. This is not to imply, however, that our appreciation of a work of art is a purely intellectual activity based on historical knowledge. If this were the case, then it would suffice to study art history; contact with a work would become irrelevant. Ultimately, our valuing of art rests on how we are affected by a work. Yet the possibility for such aesthetic response is closely connected with the kinds of factors previously outlined. It is knowledge related to technique, style, and artistic context that opens up possibilities for appreciation which go deeper than a pre-critical response; and it is factors relating to the climate of the time that inform the sensibility of an era, affecting what will speak to and touch an audience, and thus what will be appreciated and valued.

The case of innovative art might seem to be more problematic, however. Here, the works depart from the existing tradition, and often contravene or explicitly reject rules of the tradition. Thus, it may seem that these rules cannot be the basis for evaluating innovative works. We value such works because they are new and different, because they depart from the tradition. But it is not the departure alone that is important. It is the context of the innovation and the manner in which it is done which provide the basis for their value. They innovate in such a way as to provide a new and viable direction in which the art can grow, and what is viable is determined by the state of the tradition and by the state of the society. Thus works which attempt to deal with new technical problems at a point where old problems have been exhausted, or works which respond, both through form and content, to changes in society, are likely to be effective, to be appreciated, and to be valued.

It seems, then, that we value both the development of a tradition, including the exploration of the possibilities and perfection of forms entailed in the tradition, and also the departure from a tradition in a manner which facilitates development in a new direction. Thus the evaluation of artistic products is not an entirely subjective matter. The value of a work of art, even of one which is radically innovative, is not something which is intuited holistically without reference to or understanding of the tradition which gave birth to the work. Rather, the rules, techniques, and goals of the tradition provide a basis for evaluation, both in terms of the success of the work within the prevailing framework and in terms of the significance of any departure from it. Yet because the value of works of art is ultimately connected with their effect on people, the factors which determine the sensibility of an era also have a role to play in artistic value.

This view of the nature of artistic value can help to explain some of the phenomena surrounding the evaluation of works of art which are used to support the subjectivist position. One such phenomenon is the fact that artistic taste changes. Some works of art are assessed differently at different times and are more in favour at some periods than at others. This might seem to indicate that there are no objective standards for assessing works, that their value is a product of subjective preference, and this changes from era to era, and indeed, from individual to individual.

This variability in artistic evaluation can, however, be explained within the context of the view of artistic value which is being put forth here. First, it must be recognized that there is, in fact, a considerable degree of consensus in the assessment of works of art. There are works which are acknowledged masterpieces and have an almost timeless value. If a work is an outstanding and skilful example of its kind, then it will be valued as such, or if a work has broken new ground, then its place as a seminal force in a new development in the art will provide a constant basis for value. Moreover, some works, for example Michelangelo's paintings on the ceiling of the Cistine Chapel, seem to touch an aspect of humanity with fairly universal appeal, and so will have a broad and enduring basis for value.

Nonetheless, some works do rise and fall in favour at various periods, and this can likely be accounted for by the fact that what will appeal most strongly to an age will vary according to the intellectual climate of the age. The Greek classics, for example, experienced a revival in seventeenth century France, an age which has been characterized as neo-classical, and this may well have been connected with the appeal of highly structured art to an age which appreciated rules. Similarly, various ages will evaluate the same works differently. The works of Dryden and Pope, for example, were highly esteemed by the Augustans, were considered lifeless in the nineteenth century, and are once again in favour in this century.[15]

Nonetheless, this appeal of a work of art to the sensibility of an era is not a purely intuitive appeal unconnected with the rules and techniques of the tradition within which the work arises. Rather, it is an appreciation of aspects of the form and structure of the work, and so is very much based on an understanding of the techniques, rules and underlying theory of the tradition.

This analysis can also provide an explanation for the phenomenon of works of art which are not appreciated during the period in which they are created, but only later. Such works are likely shaped by factors which are beginning to influence change in art and society and are created by artists who are particularly sensitive to such factors. There is not yet sufficient distance and perspective for the significance of the innovations to be appreciated, however. Moreover, such changes would not have pervaded the society to an extent sufficient to allow for acceptance of the innovations by the contemporary audience. But at a slightly later time, the importance of the innovation in the development of the art can be assessed, and the climate has changed sufficiently for the innovation to be accepted. There is a multitude of examples of artists who were thus neglected during their lives, and only recognized a generation later and we generally consider them 'ahead of their time.'

In recognizing the links between the value of works of art and the response of an audience, the present view of artistic value might seem indistinguishable from the subjectivist position. Yet it is very different in some fundamental ways. The claim here is not that the valuing of works of art is based on immediate, subjective response, but rather that aesthetic response is crucially dependent on objective evaluations. There is a connection between the value of works and people's response because art is ultimately to be appreciated. We value it, in the end, because it can communicate to us in a special way or provide a unique type of experience. A work would simply not be valued if no one had ever been moved by it or experienced a sense of awe when confronted by it, if it had never had an impact on anyone or communicated anything, if it had never been the source of an aesthetic emotion. This does not imply, however, that the value of a work is entirely determined by the spontaneous response of an individual on a particular occasion. Such a response is affected by many factors, including mood, temperament, taste, personal experience, and knowledge, and such factors vary from individual to individual and viewing to viewing. There are many levels at which one can respond to a work, ranging from a purely subjective, spontaneous, uninformed response, to a judgment based on a great deal of knowledge of the art and of the specific framework. A work can, then, be appreciated on many different levels. One would not, I think, want to claim that the spontaneous, subjective response is totally illegitimate, but rather that with some expertise and knowledge of the art and the work, greater discrimination and another level of appreciation are possible. This deeper level of appreciation is affected by the factors which were outlined previously, and it is recognition of works of art at this level which is the basis for their lasting value.

In discussing the notion of value in art, the question may arise as to what exactly it is that is valued: is it an object, an activity, an experience? The object does seem to be important in some of the arts—painting, for example. Here there is one object, the work of art, which is the locus of value. People want to see **the** *Mona Lisa*. Reproductions are valued to some extent, as well, but not close to the extent to which the original is valued, and their value is derivative. The reproduction is a substitute for the original; it gives people an idea of the original if they do not have access to the genuine object, but it is considered vastly inferior to it. Similarly, a copy of a painting is not considered as valuable as the original and is, in fact, disdained for being a copy, a forgery, a fake.

The exclusive valuing of one object is not a characteristic of all the arts, however. For performance arts such as music and drama, there can be numerous instantiations of the work, all of which are somewhat different one from another, and each of which is highly valued. There are several reasons for this difference. In painting and the visual arts, the characteristics which produce an aesthetic experience are seen as properties of the original object. Thus a reproduction will not have the requisite aesthetic qualities. It will not have precisely the same colour values, nor can it capture the textural qualities of the original. It will be aesthetically inferior. This, in itself, does not seem to fully account for the prominent place of the original object, however. Even a copy of a painting which is extremely well done and which emulates the qualities of the original admirably—a copy which is difficult to distinguish from the original—will not be esteemed as is the original. There are, then, factors other than the purely aesthetic qualities of the work which must play a role here.[16]

One consideration is that the original painting or work of art has a value which is historical as well as aesthetic. There is awe inspired by the fact that one can have before one the very object which a reputed genius created, and this is a similar sort of awe to that which is attached to the original manuscript of a play or of a musical score, or even to the objects in a museum. Rarity is another source of value with relation to works of visual art. The original work is highly valued because it is unique, because it is one of a kind, unlike reproductions which are plentiful. Even in the case of lithographs or prints, rarity increases their value.

These factors are still not sufficient to explain how we tend to regard copies, however. There is a great deal of concern that a work be authentic, and a work which is found to be a forgery is severely condemned. We might admire the skill with which it is executed, but we condemn it for the pretense of being something which it is not. In addition to the sense of being the genuine object and not a fake, there is an additional meaning of authenticity, namely being an honest work which is a genuine product of the artist's imagination and not just produced according to a formula. These two meanings are connected, and our concern for the former seems to rest on a desire for the latter. A work which is a fake, a copy of another work, is merely imitative and cannot be a genuine product of an artist's imagination. The idea and its execution are not the producer's own, but we expect a work of art to be authentic in the second sense. This might help to explain why there is not a similar sort of problem with respect to the performing arts. A performance of a play or a piece of music is not a copy of some genuine work, but is, rather, the product of the imagination of both the playwright or composer and the particular performance artists, and is, thus, authentic in the second sense.

The importance of the imagination of the individual in our estimation of works of art can also account for our valuing of the creations of the individual over items which are mass produced. A hand-crafted pot, for example, is considered to have a kind of artistic value which a mass produced pot cannot have, since it will bear the stamp of the individual.

It has been argued to this point that there are no grounds for maintaining an extreme subjectivist position with respect to the evaluation of art. There is, in fact, a basis for the assessment of artistic products which is provided by the rules, techniques and goals of the artistic tradition and the interplay of these factors with changing social sensibilities. Even with respect to works which are highly innovative, a comparison with past products and a reference to prevailing standards must enter into their evaluation.

## *Value in Science*

The argument regarding the impossibility of objective standards for the evaluation of created products has, of late, been extended into the realm of science. The traditional view that scientific theories are assessed according to their success in accurately portraying the world has come under ever-increasing attack by philosophers of science. Some argue that there are, in fact, no objective criteria for theory choice, and that the best that we can do is to explain such choice by means of psychological and sociological factors. Some even question the rationality of the entire scientific enterprise.

The traditional view of the nature of science holds that the scientific enterprise consists in a strict method involving unbiased observation, inductive reasoning, and testing leading to a theory which can be proven, and thus to facts about the world. The criterion for the evaluation of theories is clear and straightforward: we accept a theory when it is proven according to the scientific method, and such a theory will provide an accurate representation of what the world is like.[17]

This idea that a scientific theory can be proven by the evidence gathered through observation and experimentation has come under severe attack, however. The logical problems inherent in such an inductivist account have been amply demonstrated. Hume, for example, has shown that there is no rational justification for inductive inference, that is, there are no rational grounds for accepting a hypothesis which is supported inductively over any other alternative hypothesis.[18] Thus the notion that a scientific theory can be proven by facts becomes highly questionable.

Moreover, even the notion of fact has been shown to be problematic. What we observe in a test or experiment is deemed to be a fact, and yet the very act of observing is a theory-laden activity. It involves perceptual organization which depends on previous knowledge and experience, and contains theoretical assumptions.[19] Systems of explanation are inextricably interwoven into our very observations and our recognition of facts as such, and so the distinction between fact and theory is by no means clear-cut. Lakatos makes this point with reference to Galileo's telescopic observations:

> Galileo claimed that he could 'observe' mountains on the moon and spots on the sun and that these 'observations' refuted the time-honoured theory that celestial bodies are faultless crystal balls. But his 'observations' were not 'observational' in the sense of being observed by the -unaided- senses: their reliability depended on the reliability of his telescope—and of the optical theory of the telescope—which was violently questioned by his contemporaries. It was not Galileo's - pure, untheoretical - *observations* that confronted Aristotelian *theory* but rather Galileo's 'observations' in the light of his optical theory that confronted the Aristotelians' 'observations' in the light of their theory of the heavens.[20]

Such a theoretical component of apparently factual observations is especially evident where the observation is mediated by some device or instrumentation, since these will require a theory to justify their use and reliability.

If the possibility of pure fact gleaned by observation is cast into doubt, then the claim that scientific theories can be proven by facts collapses. This problem has led some philosophers to abandon the notion of proof for scientific theories and to focus, instead, on the notion of disproof. Thus we have the falsificationist view which acknowledges the problem of induction, but attempts to rescue the empirical basis of science by maintaining that, although no number of specific instances is sufficient to prove a theory, a counter-instance is sufficient to disprove or falsify one. This view, however, is still subject to the second difficulty outlined above, given the problematic nature of facts and the impossibility of clearly distinguishing fact and theory.

Methodological falsificationism, as formulated by Popper, involves a recognition of such difficulties, but proposes a method for rationally choosing amongst theories which still maintains a connection to the empirical basis.[21] This methodology involves making a choice which is based on the results of a crucial experiment which can be specified in advance. If the results of the experiment are not as predicted, then the theory is refuted. This view avoids the problems of falsificationism outlined above because it makes no claims to actually prove or disprove a theory, but instead provides a method for choosing among theories. The difficulties of such a methodological falsificationist view have been demonstrated by numerous theorists, including Kuhn and Feyerabend.[22] Both demonstrate that methodological falsification is not, in fact, a characteristic of actual scientific practice. There are always anomalies in theories, and scientists do not abandon theories which, according to Popper's view, would be refuted. They tend to remain committed to a theory and to question the evidence and the experimental conditions, or to shore up the theory by means of auxiliary hypotheses, rather than abandoning it.

Such reasoning has led to scepticism on the part of some philosophers about the possibility of objective criteria for the choice or elimination of theories. Kuhn, for example, believes that scientific activity is characterized by a succession of paradigms and thus radical shifts in the perspective from which scientific phenomena are viewed, data are categorized, and research is organized. These paradigms are, for Kuhn, incommensurable, that is, they can be evaluated only by criteria inherent in a particular paradigm. There are no neutral standards by which they can be judged. There are, thus, no objective criteria for choosing between paradigms, and so it is largely psychological factors and consensus amongst scientists which determine which paradigm succeeds. The acceptance of a new paradigm is characterized by Kuhn as a conversion or a gestalt switch, thereby emphasizing the subjective aspect of evaluation. (This view bears a striking similarity to the subjective view of artistic value examined earlier. Both views maintain that products can be evaluated only according to criteria inherent in the relevant framework, that there are no criteria for evaluation which transcend frameworks, that frameworks are discontinuous one with another, and that the acceptance of a new product involves a subjective, intuitive grasping of novel value—a gestalt switch.)

Feyerabend goes even farther, to point out that alleged scientific method is constantly violated in actual practice, that there are metaphysical presuppositions underlying every theory, and that irrationality is, and must be, a part of scientific activity:

> Without a frequent dismissal of reason, no progress. Ideas which today form the very basis of science exist only because there were such things as prejudice, conceit, passion: because these things *opposed reason* and because they *were permitted to have their way*. We have to conclude, then, that *even within* science, reason cannot and should not be allowed to be comprehensive and that it must often be overruled, or eliminated in favour of other agencies....*Given* science, reason cannot be universal and unreason cannot be excluded.[23]

What all of these views have in common is the denial of any objective criteria for the assessment of scientific theories. Support for this perspective is derived from the fact that there is not necessarily agreement among proponents of competing theories on the standards of assessment for the theories, that there do not seem to be any standards of assessment which remain constant over time, that subjective factors are evident with respect to theory choice in actual scientific practice, and that there does not seem to be any one procedure which can be deemed to be *the* scientific method.

Even if we grant the above, does this necessarily lead to the conclusion that no objective assessment of scientific theories is possible, and that science is irrational? I think not. The traditional view that scientific theories can be proven to be true and to accurately represent the world is untenable, but this does not imply that there is no basis for assessing scientific theories. One of the grounds for asserting the impossibility of objective evaluation is the alleged discontinuity between paradigms or frameworks. If

Value 53

new paradigms are not continuations of previous paradigms but are radically different, then, it is argued, the rules and standards of the previous paradigm cannot provide the basis for evaluation of the new one. This notion of discontinuity has previously been shown to be mistaken, however. There are always continuities between theories, and such continuities provide one basis for the assessment of new theories.

Another basis for evaluation can be found in the overarching method of science, as Siegel has pointed out.[24] Siegel acknowledges that there is no one procedure or technique which can be considered to be *the* method of science, but argues that scientific method lies, rather, in its general principles of appraisal. The specific instantiations of such principles do vary over time, but a constant commitment to the evaluation of theories on the basis of such principles, a commitment to evidence is what characterizes scientific method. He states:

> ... SM [scientific method] can and should be characterized generally, as consisting in, for example, a concern for explanatory adequacy, however that adequacy is conceived; an insistence on testing, however testing is thought to be best done; and a commitment to inductive support, however inductive inference is thought to be best made. In short, changes in specific views about the construal of various aspects of SM are not sufficient to show that the aspects themselves have changed. Methodological constancy does not involve specific construals of various evaluative criteria, but rather a general commitment to such criteria, however construed.[25]

This construal of the notion of scientific method can successfully deal with the problems raised by Kuhn in his argument that there are no standards for the evaluation of scientific theories which transcend the bounds of a particular scientific paradigm. The kinds of general, methodological considerations described by Siegel provide just such standards, however. Although there may be disagreement, in debates between paradigms, about what constitutes an adequate explanation and about how evidence is to be interpreted, the necessity for explanatory adequacy and evidentiary support provide overarching standards for evaluation. Indeed, it is the existence of such standards which makes debate regarding paradigms possible, and potentially fruitful.

Another argument proposed by both Kuhn and Feyerabend against objective standards is that, in actual scientific practice, subjective factors do often enter into the process of theory choice. Even if we grant the existence of subjective factors in theory choice, however, this is not an argument against the existence of objective standards. It is always possible to ask whether the choice of a particular theory is a good one, whether a particular decision is justified, whether a particular belief is well-founded. The fact that such questions are both possible and meaningful indicates that theory choice is not reducible to subjective factors, that assessment of choices and decisions is possible, and that there are objective grounds for doing so.[26]

It appears, then, that the view that the creative products of science cannot be evaluated objectively but only subjectively in terms of some type of holistic realignment of our perceptions and worldview is unfounded. There are objective standards by which scientific products can be assessed, and these are provided both by the rules, problems, methods and criteria which are continuous between frameworks, and by the overarching methodological meta-criteria of science which transcend particular frameworks.

## *Art and Science*

We have determined, then, that the subjectivist account of value is mistaken as a description of what is involved in the valuing of creative products in both the artistic and the scientific realms. What still remains to be determined is whether there are fundamental differences between evaluation in these two spheres.

In both the artistic and scientific realms, an important basis for the assessment of products is given by the tradition itself. Both art and science exhibit gradual evolution as opposed to revolutionary transformation, and so the problems of a tradition at a particular time, and its techniques, its rules, and its methods for addressing these problems as well as its criteria for successful solution will play a role determining the value of a creative product. This is the case even for products which are highly innovative because of the considerable degree of continuity between frameworks.

In the realm of science, we have seen that there are also overarching standards for assessment which are connected with the overall nature of the scientific enterprise. The commitment to evidence which characterizes the method of science is definitive of science as a rational activity. A scientific claim, in order to be objective, must appeal to evidence, and although particular criteria of appraisal may change, this demand for evidentiary support does not.

There appears to be a parallel in the relationship between the overall nature of art and its overarching standards for evaluation. Art is concerned with aesthetic appreciation and so any judgment regarding a work of art, in order to be objective, must appeal to the aesthetic features of a work. And although particular standards for aesthetic worth may change, the requirement that works be judged according to certain aesthetic features remains constant.

One way in which evaluation in art and science may appear to differ is with respect to the role of emotion or sensibility in each domain. Our valuing of art relates to the fact that it has an effect of a certain sort on people, that it provides for aesthetic experience and aesthetic appreciation. It is not sufficient to be able to appraise a work rationally. Rather, the ultimate end of aesthetic judgment is to illuminate a work, to open it up to aesthetic appreciation.

It is important to reiterate that such a connection between artistic value and people's sensibilities in no way implies that the value of works of art is totally subjective. Aesthetic judgments do not reduce to personal preferences. Rather, they refer to objective features of works—their aesthetic properties, and to aesthetic principles. Thus it is possible for there to be assessments of works of art which are unjustified, just as there are unjustified scientific judgments. It is, then, an intimate interplay of rational judgment and sensibility which is operating in the valuing of works of art.

It may seem that evaluation in science is very different from this and that people's sensibilities are not involved in the same way. Yet the picture of science as strictly rational, cold, and unemotional is a considerably impoverished one. While the evaluation of scientific theories is ultimately governed by rational criteria, these assessments are not without an emotive component. Goodman makes this point in discussing the importance of discernment by feeling:

> in any science, while the requisite objectivity forbids wishful thinking, prejudicial reading of evidence, rejection of unwanted

results, avoidance of ominous lines of inquiry, it does not forbid use of feeling in exploration and discovery, the impetus of inspiration and curiosity, or the cues given by excitement over intriguing problems and promising hypotheses.[27]

Moreover, sensibilities are centrally involved in science in the form of the aesthetic criteria which affect theory choice. Scientists frequently maintain that when other considerations are of equal weight, aesthetic considerations such as simplicity, elegance, unity and beauty play a decisive role.[28] This does not mean that theory choice reduces to subjective factors, however, but rather that rational and emotional factors are not always easily separated.

Another possible difference in the basis for value in the two areas is with respect to the notion of progress. Because we tend to think of science as aiming at an increasing understanding of the world (some may even say truth), we expect scientific theories to provide ever better explanations—we expect science to progress. The aim of artistic activity, however, is appreciation, and so it is not progress which is at issue, but rather the opening up of new possibilities for appreciation.

It might be objected, here, that this distinction is too strong, and that the notion of progress is equally applicable to art as to science. Yet there are important differences between the way the notion can be applied in the two areas. A case can, perhaps, be made for the claim that there can be progress in art within a framework. A framework will embody a set of goals, rules, and techniques, and the techniques might improve over time to better meet the goals. The notion of progress does not seem to be as applicable between frameworks, however. It does not seem to be the case that works of art have necessarily improved over time, but rather, that new possibilities have been explored and there are new works which can be appreciated. In science, a new theory must in some sense be better than its predecessors in order to be valued. It must encompass them, explain all that they can and more. A new school of art does not have to encompass the previous one in this way, however. It will include what came before in the sense that it presupposes it and has grown out of it, and it is, thus, meaningful to speak of development in art. But it does not have to do what the previous style did and more. Rather, it will do something different. One would not, I think, want to say, for example, that Impressionist landscapes did what previous landscapes did and more. Rather, they were attempting something different. They might seem to achieve an advance in terms of portraying the effects of light, but at the same time they lost some of the imitative accuracy of detail. It is true that this type of loss can also occur between successive scientific theories, but nevertheless the new theory must exhibit some type of overall superiority over the old one. This is not the case in art. There is not a linear progression in art, but rather, new styles add new ways of seeing and portraying to our repertoire. They add new possibilities, whose value is a reflection of numerous factors.

It might be argued, however, that art can exhibit progress in terms of becoming truer to life, and that there is, thus, an empirical basis for value in art as there is in science. It may seem, for example, that a painting can represent a landscape or a person with varying degrees of accuracy, and that a more accurate representation would be truer to reality and thus more valuable. This notion of art as representing reality is problematic, however. Art cannot really copy reality. It can only transpose it. Any work of art is a creation of the artist's imagination in which the world is transformed according to the artist's perceptions, subjective feelings, techniques, and aesthetic principles. Thus a work sometimes allows us to see a new aspect of a subject, and in such cases we might feel that a work is somehow true. This does not mean that this particular rendition is necessarily truer than another, however, but rather, that we recognize and can relate to this aspect of the subject. The truth of a work, if it makes sense to refer to truth at all in this context, is emotional, based on what is evoked, and not really pictorial. Thus it refers to an aspect of how we view a subject, and different works can refer to different aspects. There is not some overriding criterion of truth according to which works could be measured. As Gombrich states, "The truth of a landscape is relative."[29] The notion of progress is inapplicable to art because there is no standard goal to which all works aspire, nor could there be. Thus there is no standard of progress. In science, however, such a standard is continually sought and considered vital to the entire scientific enterprise.

Kuhn denies that such a standard is possible even in the realm of science, and so rejects the notion of cumulative scientific progress. He admits that there can be progress within a paradigm, since the problems, techniques, and modes of solution are specified.

Revolutionary science, however, is characterized by the succession of a new paradigm which brings with it a new set of problems, categories and concepts. Thus it is not a question of the new paradigm being an improvement over the old in the sense of achieving more of the same. Rather, it will do something somewhat different. Furthermore, this succession of paradigms cannot, according to Kuhn, be viewed as a process of getting closer to the truth. It will exhibit a type of growth, but this growth is not toward a specific goal.

Kuhn's account of scientific growth has much in common with the view of artistic development outlined above. For both views, progress is possible within a framework, but between frameworks the situation is more complex. Different frameworks cannot be compared in terms of any overriding criteria, and so, when a new framework is accepted, it is not a question of linear, cumulative progress but rather of development or growth.

There are a number of problems with Kuhn's view. First, it rests on the radical distinction between normal science and revolutionary science, but this distinction has previously been shown to be untenable. There are continuities between successive theories in terms of problems, methods and criteria, and these provide grounds for determining whether a new theory offers an improvement over an older one. Moreover, standards for assessing progress are provided by the methodological meta-criteria outlined above. Indeed, it would seem that Kuhn himself could hardly avoid acknowledging this possibility. He does see the process of science as characterized by "an increasingly detailed and refined understanding of nature"[30] and there would have to be standards for assessing whether new theories were providing an understanding which was, in fact, more detailed and more refined.

Thus the difference between art and science with respect to the notion of progress does seem to hold. There is no requirement that a new artistic development provide "an increasingly detailed and refined understanding of nature." It need not provide a more adequate explanation of nature, nor be better supported by evidence than its predecessor. It need not do what its predecessor has done and more. Rather, it provides new possibilities for appreciation, although there are considerable constraints regarding what will constitute viable and valuable possibilities.

## Summary

In the course of this chapter we have confronted the view that there are no objective criteria for the evaluation of creations, and that an appeal must be made to subjective factors in order to explain our valuing of novel products. It has been argued that this view rests on an erroneous belief in the discontinuity between created works and their antecedents. There are, in fact, continuities with preceding aspects of the tradition even for works which are highly innovative, and these provide one basis for the evaluation of creative products in both art and science. It is the overall aims of the tradition, its fundamental problems and guiding methodology which determine the significance of both artistic and scientific creations, although there are differences between the artistic and scientific traditions which account for some differences in modes of evaluation in these two domains.

### NOTES

1. Immanuel Kant, *The Critique of Judgment*, J.C. Meredith, trans. (Oxford: Oxford University Press, 1952).
2. Hausman, *Discourse on Novelty*, p.51.
3. Kuhn, *Structure of Scientific Revolutions*.
4. Paul Feyerabend, *Against Method* (London: NLB, 1975).
5. Kuhn has at times denied that his view is radically subjective, eg. in his "Objectivity, Value Judgment, and Theory Choice," in T. Kuhn, *The Essential Tension* (Chicago: University of Chicago Press, 1977). It has, however, been demonstrated that a consistent interpretation of Kuhn's view necessarily leads to the radical subjectivity thesis. See I. Scheffler, *Science and Subjectivity* (Indianapolis: Hackett Publishing Company, 1982); H. Siegel, "Objectivity, Rationality, Incommensurability and More," *British Journal for the Philosophy of Science* 31, 4, 1980.
6. Herbert Read, *Education Through Art* (London: Faber and Faber, 1946); Suzanne Langer, *Feeling and Form* (New York: Charles Scribner's Sons, 1953).
7. Clive Bell, *Art* (New York: Capricorn Books, 1958), pp.15-34.
8. Ibid., p.27. He says, for example, "The representative element in a work of art may or may not be harmful; always it is irrelevant."
9. Ernst Kris, *Psychoanalytic Explorations in Art* (New York: International Universities Press, 1952), p.21.
10. Frederick S. Wight, *The Potent Image* (New York: Collier Books, 1976), p.115.

11. Igor Stravinsky, *Poetics of Music* (New York: Vintage Books, 1947), pp.58-59.

12. E.H. Gombrich, *Art and Illusion* (Princeton: Princeton University Press, 1969), p.65.

13. Wight, *Potent Image*, p.70.

14. Grout, *Western Music*, p.653.

15. Jerome Stolnitz, *Aesthetics and Philosophy of Art Criticism* (Boston: Houghton Mifflin Company, 1960), p.393.

16. Nelson Goodman claims that the fact that it may be extremely difficult to distinguish between a forgery and an original painting does not alter the fact that the difference between them is aesthetic because knowledge of the difference will affect the manner in which the two paintings are and will be perceived. *Languages of Art* (Indianapolis: Hackett Publishing Company, 1976), pp.99-112.

17. See, for example, C.G. Hempel, *Philosophy of Natural Science* (Englewood Cliffs, N.J.: Prentice-Hall, 1966).

18. David Hume, *Treatise of Human Nature*, Book 1, ed. D.G.C. Macnabb (London: Wm. Collins Sons and Co., 1962; first published 1739), part iii, section vi.

19. See, for example, N.R. Hanson, *Patterns of Discovery* (Cambridge: Cambridge University Press, 1958).

20. Imre Lakatos, *The Methodology of Scientific Research Programmes* (Cambridge: Cambridge University Press, 1978), pp.14-15; Cf. Feyerabend, *Against Method*, sections 9-11.

21. Karl Popper, *The Logic of Scientific Discovery* (New York: Harper and Row, Publishers, 1968).

22. Kuhn, *Structure of Scientific Revolutions*; Feyerabend, *Against Method*.

23. Feyerabend, *Against Method*, pp.179-180.

24. Harvey Siegel, "What Is the Question Concerning the Rationality of Science?" *Philosophy of Science* 52, 4, 1985.

25. Ibid., p.528.

26. See Siegel, "Objectivity, Rationality, Incommensurability and More."

27. Goodman, *Languages of Art*, p.248.

28. See, for example, P.A.M. Dirac, "The Evolution of the Physicist's Picture of Nature," *Scientific American* 5, 1963: 47; W. Heisenberg, *Physics and Beyond* (New York: Harper and Row, 1971), p.68.

29. Gombrich, *Art and Illusion*, p.49.

30. Kuhn, *Structure of Scientific Revolutions*, p.170.

# Chapter III

# PRODUCT, PROCESS, PERSON

THE WAY of thinking about creativity which is characteristic of contemporary psychological and educational theory has been marked by a move away from an emphasis on the production of valuable products and has stressed, instead, the creative process and also the creative person. This rejection of the connection between creativity and the production of valuable products is due, in part, to the notion that there are no criteria for determining which products are, in fact, valuable. Furthermore, there is an assumption implicit in this view that there is a distinctive creative process and that this process differs radically from ordinary, logical thinking. While the latter is seen to be methodical, convergent, rule-bound and highly judgmental, the former is viewed as divergent, spontaneous, and generative, involving the suspension of judgment, leaps of imagination, rule-breaking and irrational processes. A corollary of this view is that some individuals are better able to engage in this process than others because of their cognitive and personality traits, and so creativity is viewed as a quality possessed by a person regardless of whether the person actually creates anything.

In this chapter, the application of the notion of creativity to products, processes and persons will be examined. It has previously been shown that the view that there are no criteria for the assessment of creative products is mistaken. Here it will be argued that there is not a distinctive creative process which is different from our ordinary processes of thought, and that there are consequent problems with the derivative notion of a distinctive creative personality. Thus, the only coherent way in which to view creativity is in terms of the production of valuable products.

## *Product*

A debate between J.P. White and M.J. Parsons[1] exemplifies clearly opposing views about the nature of creativity; the contrast provided by these views lays bare some basic issues concerning the use of the term 'creativity' and its cognates. White claims that the term does not have one meaning which applies to an inner process, but instead has a variety of meanings depending on the specific circumstances of its application. He maintains that 'creative' is an evaluative term, one which we use to praise a person's achievements. Thus, for White, the ascription of creativity is dependent upon the production of a product. Furthermore, the product must be deemed valuable, and this can only be assessed according to the criteria of the specific discipline. 'Creativity' is, thus, not a general term which can be applied unqualified, but is specific to an area.

What White is denying is that 'creative' is in any sense a psychological term which refers to an inner process. It is, he claims, rather, the fact that certain individuals produced works which we value which prompts us to call them creative. According to White, we have no way of determining whether there is a specific thought process common to all the instances where we attribute creativity. But, even if there were, this would not be relevant. It is in virtue of what is produced that we attribute creativity. Thus he says:

> Creative thinking...is not a peculiar type of thinking that has different, non-publicly observable, features from other types of thinking. A creative thinker is one whose thinking leads to a result which conforms to criteria of value in one domain or another. 'Creative' is a medal which we pin on public products, not the name of private processes.[2]

Parsons, on the other hand, argues that the primary sense of creativity is connected, not with works, but with persons. He assents to White's description of 'creative' as it applies to works, but claims that this use does not preclude it being predicated of persons and processes as well. As applied to persons, he claims it means, not that a person has produced valuable works, but rather, that the person is capable of doing so. The production of works would provide evidence for our belief that a person possesses this capacity, but it is the capacity and not the works to which we refer and which are of primary interest when attributing creativity. It might, therefore, make sense to call someone creative who had never produced a valuable work, for this person might, nonetheless, have the capacity to do so.

Moreover, Parsons maintains that the capacity to be creative involves the ability to engage in a specific mental process. He disagrees with White that one cannot speak meaningfully of mental processes, but argues that they can be described in non-private ways. One could, for example, compare the procedures and techniques employed by two individuals and surmise, if these were seen to be the same, that they were thinking in the same way and thus engaging in similar mental processes.

Numerous issues are raised in the course of this debate. The first of these centres on the relationship between creativity and a product. Certainly the root meaning of the verb is connected with a product. To create is to make or bring into being something which did not exist previously, or at least not in that form. It would not make sense to say that a person created if nothing is produced. This is especially apparent in the case of art. One creates in art by making in a medium. It is not the case that a work is created in the mind and subsequently executed. Such a conception-execution distinction is inappropriate to artistic creation. Rather, creating takes place by actually doing—by painting, by writing, by composing. Now it may sometimes be the case, in poetry for example, that one creates in one's mind before actually executing the work, that is, before writing down the poem, but this does not seem to be an instance of creating without a product. Rather, the poet has in fact created a poem by working it out through the medium of language, but has simply not committed it to paper. Thus, this would not be a case of creating unconnected with a product.

What is the relationship, however, between our ascriptions of creativity and the production of a product? Parsons argues that the primary sense of 'creative' relates to persons without reference to products, and that a person could be creative without ever creating anything. This argument presupposes that there is a capacity to create which individuals might possess irrespective of whether they actually do create anything, and that it is this capacity which is the object of reference and of interest in talking about creativity. The question of whether such a capacity could, in fact, exist, and whether it even makes sense to talk about creative capacity will be dealt with later.

At this point, however, let us question the claim that a connection to a product is not fundamental, even to a view such as Parsons's. First, even if a creative capacity existed, how would it be possible to know whether a person possessed such a capacity? If someone produces valuable works, then we can, of course, say in retrospect that she was capable of producing valuable works, that she had the capacity to do so. If she has not done so, however, then what would lead one to attribute to her a creative capacity? Perhaps she has created valuable works in the past. In this case, the production of a product in the past is the basis for the prediction of future production. Is there any way of establishing a creative capacity in the case where a person has never created a valuable work, however? It might be claimed that this could be established through psychological tests and assessments of various types. There is, however, no obvious logical connection between performance on tests and creating a work, nor has there yet been established any verifiable empirical connection. But more on this later. Ultimately, the only accurate indicator of alleged creative capacity would be the production of a valuable work.

Moreover, despite Parsons's claim that it is creative capacity which is the notion of primary interest, the notion of product does seem to be central to his account. One important reason for interest in alleged creative capacity is the desire to foster the production of products. One is not interested, from an educational standpoint, solely in fostering such a capacity for its own sake. Certainly I do not think that Parsons would be satisfied if we could somehow succeed in producing a generation of individuals who possessed a capacity to create (however this could be determined) but who never created anything. The notion of capacity is of educational interest largely because it provides a focus for investigating means to foster the creation of products. It is considered desirable that people create valuable works of art, scientific theories, technological innovations, and solutions to social problems and so we postulate something in common amongst those who create so that we can investigate whether such production can be fostered.

## *Process*

The idea that creativity is primarily to be viewed as a characteristic of persons rests on the claim that there is a distinctive process which characterizes creating. There have been numerous attempts to describe the nature of such a putative process. Two such accounts will be described in some detail here.

Arthur Koestler[3] offers an account of the creative process which has been quite influential. He explains the act of creation in terms of a coming together of two realms of thought which had previously been considered incompatible—a bisociation of unconnected matrices, in his terminology. According to this view, humour, science, and art are all a product of the same type of process, the difference depending on the nature of the coming together and the emotional response evoked. When the matrices clash, humour, with its accompanying aggressive tendencies, is the result. A juxtaposition produces art, which elicits self-transcending emotions, and scientific discovery is a result of the synthesis of the two realms of thought and involves both emotions.

The concept of habit plays a key role in Koestler's theory. He stresses the hierarchical nature of the organization of the brain, in which a skill, once learned, is taken over by lower centres and thereby becomes mechanized to a great extent. Repetition through largely unchanging conditions produces rigid patterns or habits which become difficult to break. This applies not only to motor skills but also to patterns of thought. Through repetition and experience, patterns of mental organization are established which direct the mind to the data which are deemed relevant to any particular idea, or in other words, to the relevant matrix.

Such habits are essential in order to organize experience and maintain stability and ordered behaviour, but they can also be an impediment to any new forms of thought. The difficulty occurs when the matrix under consideration will not yield the solution to the problem and becomes blocked. It is here that creative thought comes into play, for it is necessary to go beyond the matrix in question, and connect it with another which was previously thought of as irrelevant or unconnected. This process is such a difficult one because it has a destructive as well as a constructive component. It is necessary to break firmly entrenched habits and to disrupt rigid patterns of mental organization. Once this occurs, however, the two matrices become inseparably fused and result in a new production.

According to Koestler, the unconscious plays a crucial role in this process. In this mode of thought, the shackles of ordinary logic with its inherent preconceptions are loosened, permitting the free play of ideas and the occurrence of unlikely combinations.

Although Koestler does lay considerable stress upon the element of novelty, he does recognize the role of conscious, deliberate, convergent thought for creativity, and in fact, stresses the importance of such 'ripeness' in order for discovery to be possible. In order for the creative process to take place, each of the matrices which will eventually come together must be well established and exercised. This involves extensive advanced preparation and subsequent conscious elaboration and verification. The divergent element, the creative leap, can take place only within the framework of such convergent thought.

Another influential analysis of the creative process is given by Edward De Bono.[4] He claims that there are two basic modes of thinking which exist, vertical thinking and lateral thinking, and he draws a sharp distinction between the two. The former is used in logical thinking to solve type problems and to check the reasonableness of solutions. It is the sort of thinking which one uses most frequently for problem-solving, and involves remaining rigidly within a given framework and thinking along established paths. Moreover, it is essentially selective, judging what is produced according to the criteria of prevailing patterns. Lateral thinking, on the other hand, is strictly generative, producing new ideas without evaluating them, and is, thus, characterized by a suspension of judgment. It involves going outside the framework for the solution to a problem or for an idea which will lead to a solution, and making leaps between established paths and new connections among them. De Bono argues that we tend to become inflexible in our patterned way of thinking, and that lateral thinking involves recognizing the arbitrariness of our conventional categories and looking at phenomena in a new way, thereby overcoming the limitations of vertical thinking. He further claims that one can acquire the skill of lateral thinking through practice, and the techniques which he suggests to this end include deliberately trying many approaches to a problem, consciously reversing relationships, forming analogies, accepting absurd ideas, play, brainstorming, shifting emphasis, and random stimulation of ideas.

These two accounts have many features in common and express what are, in essence, quite similar views about the nature of the creative process. They both affirm, first, that there is a distinct process which characterizes creativity, and that this process is essentially the same regardless of subject matter. They both maintain that most thinking is confined within specific frameworks and is marked by rigidity and habit and that this creative process involves breaking out of such habitual ways of thinking and disrupting existing patterns of thought. It further involves making new connections between previously unrelated entities by performing a leap of some sort. Both accounts hold that this process is not strictly rational, but involves elements of chance and unconscious processes which loosen the hold of conventional logic. Finally, this process is seen, in both views, as non-evaluative and involving a suspension of judgment, although it is recognized that acts of judgment may precede and follow the actual creative act. Although derived from the views of Koestler and De Bono, these basic features are, in fact, common to most of the accounts of creative process.

Let us begin to examine this basic view by looking at the idea that creativity is characterized by a specific way of thinking which is different from our usual logical way of thinking. I would object that this view draws an artificial distinction between creative and non-creative thinking and that the two are, in fact, neither clearly distinct nor easily separable. This view distinguishes between two such ways of thinking on the grounds that logical thinking is selective, is confined to frameworks and established patterns, and involves judgment whereas creative thinking is purely generative and involves the disruption of established patterns and the suspension of judgment. I would maintain, however, that thinking of all kinds involves a combination of both types of processes, and that, in fact, they are not easily separated.

The model of the creative process advocated by the preceding theorists appears to be along the following lines: one is faced with a problem, one suspends judgment and generates new possibilities by the use of disruptive elements (one thinks creatively), and finally, one reinstitutes judgment and evaluates the products thus produced. I would argue, however, that judgment is intimately involved throughout the process of creating. The initial perception of the problem as a problem and the determining of the general direction for solution are very much products of judgment. It is because one has considerable expertise in an area and is immersed in its intricacies that one develops the judgment that enables one to see a certain concatenation of phenomena as in need of exploration or explanation, to see it as a problem.

Moreover, the need for a disruption of established patterns is connected with judgment, as well. Theories such as those outlined previously base much of their speculation on the single fact that, during the process of creating, we do sometimes suspend one or more of the presuppositions with which we began. Extrapolating from this fact, they emphasize the shaking up of established patterns as the prime characteristic of the creative process, and claim that such a disruption cannot be governed by judgment since its effects would be inhibiting. I would claim, however, that such a departure from established patterns, when it does occur, is not totally free and generated by random external stimuli, but is governed by many parameters. When presuppositions are questioned in real situations, it is not normally as a result of a random shakeup of ideas, but is, rather, because one is led to do this as a result of the stage reached in the exploration of a problem. One's thinking to this point indicates the necessity to question a presupposition in order to arrive at a solution.

One of the reasons why it is believed that judgment cannot be involved in the creative process is connected with the picture of the creative act as spontaneous. The idea is that one cannot be engaged in a process which is creative if one can foresee the outcome of one's activity. According to this view, such foresight would imply a complete plan and would thus preclude the spontaneity which is considered to be characteristic of the creative act.[5] Since judgment is viewed according to this theory as applicable only within the context of an activity where there is a plan and an end in view, it is concluded that judgment cannot enter into the creative process.

Howard argues, however, that this view, which he calls the "Unforeseen Theory of Creativity"[6] is based on a confusion about what it means to foresee an outcome. It is probably true that one does not know exactly what the end product will be like when one begins to create. Nonetheless, it does seem that one can have at least some general or vague idea of the form which this end product will take. According to Howard:

> For even if it be argued that one never *knows* what one will do in advance of doing it, one may yet *intend* in greater or lesser detail to do this or that and know one's intention perfectly well. Only that is required to 'foresee' what one undertakes to create; not a prediction, or clairvoyance, still less full knowledge of results.[7]

One begins with some sort of intention—to solve a problem, to try and execute a work, or simply to experiment in a medium, and one must know when a solution has been achieved or a work completed. Not just any combinations will be generated, but only those which might contribute to the work. Poincaré gives a good statement of this point with reference to mathematical invention:

To create consists precisely in not making useless combinations and in making those which are useful and which are only a small minority. Invention is discernment, choice.[8]

This point can be illustrated with some examples. The first involves one of De Bono's own examples in which he recounts how he used the technique of random stimulation to help solve the problem of teacher shortages in Nigeria.[9] He had introduced the randomly generated word 'tadpole' into a discussion of teacher training, and this had given rise to the idea of giving the teachers 'tails', or apprentices, who could be trained quickly. It must be recognized, however, that such a technique is effective only if there are constraints operating as to the form of the solution. The trigger word 'tadpole' did not give rise to such ideas as giving each teacher a tadpole or training tadpoles as teachers. The proffered solution had to meet certain criteria, and only those ideas which conformed to these criteria would be seen as even potential solutions. There is judgment operating here to determine which ideas might be fruitful as solutions to a problem, and even what kind of ideas would count as solutions.

This point can be illustrated further by means of a typical De Bono problem, that of the creation of a specified geometric shape out of specific constituent pieces, where there is a common assumption which must be overcome in order to arrive at the solution. In the case of this type of problem, the form of the solution is most definitely known in advance — a certain geometric shape arrived at by rearranging the pieces. The area in which the solution to such a problem will occur is very strictly delineated by the nature of the problem, and some potential solutions are simply unacceptable. Neither taking a scissors and cutting the shapes to fit nor imagining that the shapes are made of wax and can be melted down and reshaped would be considered as appropriate solutions to this problem. It is true that there is one assumption which must be discarded in order to arrive at the solution (in this example it is the assumption that the pieces must be used in the order in which they are presented), and so too narrow a preconception of the problem might prove to be inhibiting. Nonetheless, some preconceptions about the nature of the problem and the range of possible solutions are essential in order even to begin to think about the problem, let alone to have a reasonable chance of arriving at a solution.

The experience of writing poetry may provide yet another illustration of this point. As Howard points out, the Unforeseen Theory of Creativity has had a great deal of influence on thinking about artistic creation. Collingwood, for example, stresses the idea that an artist does not know what precisely it is he wants to express before he begins to create, but that he works this out in the process of execution.[10] Now we can grant Collingwood that the artist may not preconceive the precise form and details of the finished work, but nonetheless, he will begin with something—a vague feeling, a desire, an intention, an experiment, and his skill—according to which choices are made. He will not know precisely what the work will look like, but he must know when he has arrived at a result which is satisfactory. Moreover, what he brings with him to the work will play a role in determining the possibilities which are generated. Let us take, as an example, a poet attempting to find a unique and non-cliché simile for her feelings of love. The picture which De Bono's account seems to evoke is of the poet generating, in an unrestrained manner, as many combinations of ideas as possible, perhaps aided by some random stimulation such as looking around the room. By such a technique, she might arrive at some remarkable and certainly novel similes—perhaps love is like a messy desk, or my longing is like an old typewriter—but these will have very little relationship to what she really wants to say. In actual cases of artistic creation, even the possibilities which are generated are directed by what the artist brings to the work and governed by artistic judgment.

David Perkins cites an example of the thinking of a poet during the process of creating a poem which paints a picture quite different from the above. The poet had begun with the lines, "My babies are wailing like those air raid drills/ I remember." Here is how she recounts her thoughts at trying to end the poem:

> Well, I was thinking (reads) 'and I am still fighting that cold war/ alone'. The wailing babies—what did they signal for me to do? And actually, (pause) why do you hide? It's because you're trying to preserve yourself, and that's what the babies are signaling me to do, too, because basically I can't, I don't tolerate them very well, and it does me in so much that I have to leave them and go into silence someplace that's silent so I can preserve myself.[11]

Rather than the random generation of possibilities, this poet's thinking displays reasoning, logic, and considerable judgment.

This idea that judgment is suspended during the process of creating seems to be based on a particular view of the role of judgment in thought. It is assumed that judgment can be applied only within a specified framework, but that in creative thought the presuppositions of a framework are abandoned and so there can no longer be any criteria according to which one can judge.

Some of the problems with this conception have already been examined. Old presuppositions are never all abandoned, nor could they be. It is sometimes the case that one or more assumptions must be rejected in the process of arriving at a creation. Some elements of the previous framework must remain, however, elements in light of which the new structure will make sense and be fruitful. If all presuppositions were abandoned, the result would not be creation but chaos. Perkins makes this point well:

> the fact remains that no one can depart from much of the preselection at once and expect to make progress. The mathematician cannot discard the familiar axioms *and* conventional notation *and* traditions about which sorts of questions are worthwhile *and* the usual format for proofs....What we perceive as revolutionary innovation in a field always challenges only a little of the preselection. Only because we focus on the contrast rather than the continuity does innovation seem so much of a departure.[12]

This point can be illustrated with respect to Einstein's theory of relativity. This discovery is frequently cited as a prime instance of the destruction of an existing framework and the overturning of presuppositions. Yet it was Einstein's commitment to the presupposition that the laws of physics are invariant which necessitated his ultimate abandonment of the presupposition of absolute time. Some presuppositions must remain, some elements of the existing structure which give meaning to the enterprise and according to which judgments can be made.

This view that the creative process involves the suspension of judgment also makes certain assumptions about the nature of frameworks and the way they function in thinking which are highly suspect. It assumes that ordinary thinking takes place within rigidly bounded and highly rule-governed frameworks. Within these frameworks, all necessary information is given, and the mode of thinking required is analytic and evaluative, involving judgments made almost mechanically according to the logic of the framework. Given this picture of frameworks, it would seem to follow that a radically different type of thinking is required to transcend frameworks, a type of thinking which suspends the criteria of judgment of the framework, which breaks rules, which makes irrational leaps, and which generates novelty.

This view of how frameworks operate is mistaken, however. One source of this inaccuracy is the construal of the notion of framework as clearly defined and rigidly bounded. In actuality, there are only a very limited number of cases in which we operate within clear-cut, clearly determined, and rigidly bounded frameworks. The game of chess would be one example. Here the information relevant to the enterprise is strictly delimited, and any other knowledge or information is outside the framework. Even in this case, however, there is scope for creativity in terms of the specific strategies undertaken. Although, in one sense, the game is totally circumscribed by rules in terms of the specifications for legitimate moves, the possibilities for actual manoeuvres in a dynamic game are wide open.

In most instances of problem-solving and of creation, however, the notion of a rigid and precisely determined framework is even less applicable. What precisely would be the framework which is involved in the writing of a poem about the poet's experience of war, or in attempts to solve the unemployment problem? There are factors which would be relevant in each case, for example the conventions of poetry in the former case or the prevailing economic models in the latter. But there are many additional sorts of factors which might be relevant, as well. The poet's anger at the belligerence of a colleague might, for example, be relevant to how he frames his poem, or an individual's sense of compassion might be part of the framework determining her approach to an economic problem. In most problem-solving or creative situations, it would be difficult to strictly circumscribe the domain of those factors which are relevant, which constitute the framework. In actual cases, frameworks overlap, shift, and have indefinite boundaries.

Even within traditional disciplines, one is not dealing with static and rigid bodies of information. Rather, disciplines are open-ended and dynamic. They involve not merely information, but also live questions and modes of investigating these questions. And even the body of facts is not fixed but is in flux. Thus the rigid framework model is not accurate even within disciplinary areas.

This fluid aspect of frameworks is even more apparent in interdisciplinary and real life problem contexts. In such situations, relevant considerations are seldom confined to one framework, but involve, rather, information from a variety of perspectives and frames of reference. As Paul states with reference to such real life problems:

> We cannot justifiably assume that any one frame of reference or point of view is pre-eminently correct, as the perspective within which these basic human problems are to be most rationally settled.[13]

The very notion of a clearly defined framework has limited applicability in such contexts. What, for example, would be the framework for thinking about questions regarding war and peace or concerning love and human relationships? Thus the idea that most of our thinking takes place within clearly defined and rigidly bounded frameworks is largely a misconception.

Tied in with the notion of rigid frameworks is the idea of creative leaps, but this notion is problematic, as well. If frameworks were rigid and clearly defined, then some sort of extraordinary leap would be required in order to get beyond a framework. If we construe frameworks in a more fluid manner, however, then the case for leaps is considerably weakened. Creation and discovery can be seen to involve a more gradual process than the creative process model would suggest. Although they often involve moments of insight and overturning presuppositions to see things differently, these can be understood as features of a reasonable process, rather than as manifestations of an irrational, inexplicable leap.

Let us take, as an example, Galileo's adoption of the Copernican model of planetary organization. The popular view seems to be that, through a flash of insight, Galileo made a leap to see motion as relative, thus abandoning the presupposition of absolute motion, and he could then recognize the truth of the Copernican view. It is plausible to argue, however, that there were many factors which contributed to Galileo's eventual acceptance of Copernicanism, and that, in view of these factors, the process can be seen to be entirely reasonable. First, factors of personality likely contributed to his psychological readiness to accept the view, since his independence and contentiousness made him temperamentally disposed to reject authority. In addition, his home environment doubtless predisposed him to have faith in sensory evidence since his father was one of the first to perform experiments in music and believed that sensory evidence was to be given credence over authority. Furthermore, both his own work in terrestrial physics and some prior theories likely paved the way by providing conceptual antecedents, the theory of optical relativity foreshadowing the notion of relativity of motion and impetus theory facilitating the acceptance of an inertial concept. Moreover, the Copernican view seemed to him to provide the possibility of a physical explanation for an unexplained terrestrial phenomenon, the tides. Finally, Galileo was confronted with supporting evidence, in the form of telescopic observations which he had no reason to doubt.[14] According to this account, then, the notion of a conceptual leap is minimized. Rather than being a case of leaping outside a framework, Galileo's thinking seems to be characterized by extending notions and widening the domain of their applicability, in this case extending the domain of terrestrial physics to celestial phenomena.

This phenomenon of seeing things in a broader context, of getting an overall picture, of overcoming blocks to solve a problem, is not a rare occurrence, but is a feature of thinking well in general. As Jerome Bruner suggests, going beyond the information given is an important aspect of how we think, and is not limited to instances of creation.[15] Rather than postulating some extraordinary process to account for creation, then, creativity can be seen in terms of the processes which allow us to 'go beyond the information given' in all of our intelligent thought and behaviour. Creative thinking is not, then, mysterious and different from everyday thinking, but can be accounted for in terms of the processes which constitute all our thinking. Thus everyday thinking and creative thinking are not different in kind but merely in degree.

This account of the process of creating is substantiated by the research of both Weisberg[16] and Perkins.[17] Weisberg found no evidence of divergent thinking, unconscious processes, or leaps of insight in either his own empirical studies of individuals solving problems, in his analyses of the methods and products of creative 'geniuses', or in his examination of other empirical studies. Rather, the evidence he gathered seems to indicate that creative thinking is incremental in nature, involving a step by step procedure of modification of previous ideas based on increased information.

## Product, Process, Person 75

Perkins's work leads to similar conclusions. Through the use of first person accounts of individuals engaged in creative endeavours, as well as by making use of the psychological literature on the subject, he demonstrates how phenomena such as noticing, recognizing, searching, remembering, and evaluating can, together, contribute to a creative result.

He shows, for example, how the phenomenon of insight and the feeling of having made a mental leap can be accounted for in terms of the processes of recognizing and realizing, both of which constitute part of our everyday repertoire for understanding. These processes involve filling in information beyond what is directly given, thus giving the illusion of a leap. Noticing is another everyday process which plays a role in creating. This type of recognition in which one's attention is not directly focussed on a specific makes possible scanning for multiple targets when one is searching or trying to solve a problem, picking out difficulties in the process of evaluation, and recognizing opportunities in a work in progress which facilitate further developments.

He demonstrates, as well, how creating is facilitated by remembering. What we recall is not random, but is directed by numerous constraints, both explicit and implicit. The fact that we are able to recall an idea which will meet multiple criteria provides the explanation for how we are able to search effectively—of how, for example, a poet can come up with the right word without examining myriad alternatives.

He also shows, by means of examples such as the poet at work cited earlier, as well as the solving of 'insight' problems, that creative enterprises sometimes take place precisely through the use of reasoning. The feeling of sudden enlightenment which often accompanies insight does not necessarily indicate that reasoning has been by-passed, because reason itself can be either slow and deliberate or quick and spontaneous.

It is frequently maintained that the principal block to creating lies in the failure to examine a sufficient number of alternatives, or premature closure as it is called in the psychological literature, and that increased fluency in generating ideas is linked to creative production. Perkins's examination revealed no such link, however. In a study of poets, he found that the most highly rated poets, although they tended to score well on fluency tests, did not, in the actual act of composing, search through many alternatives, but usually considered only one or two options. Perkins concludes that there is a quality-quantity trade-off operating, that is, that people can either come up with numerous solutions of lower quality or few solutions of higher quality, but that they have difficulty generating both quantity and quality. He argues, then, that the problem of inadequacy of solutions stems, not from lack of fluency, but rather from insufficiently clear and high standards to begin with.

The studies of both Perkins and Weisberg support my contention that extraordinary means are not necessary in order to achieve extraordinary ends, but that it is, rather, the skill with which ordinary thinking processes are used and the purpose to which they are put which enable outstanding results to be achieved. This assimilation of creative thinking with everyday thinking does not demean the nature of creativity. Rather, it suggests that what is special about creativity lies in what is achieved rather than in how it is achieved, that it concerns product more than process.

The argument to this point suggests that there is not one unique process which characterizes creating. Rather, we employ a variety of processes, processes which are not specific to creative activity but which are intrinsic to all our thinking. Moreover different types of creative activities may call forth to various extents different processes and so the nature of the individual endeavour is important in determining how creating happens. The specific discipline and the characteristics of the particular work impose constraints and we develop skills and judgment which relate to these constraints.

We have seen, then, that creativity is not characterized by a process in terms of a distinctive mode of thought which is different from ordinary thinking. It has been claimed, however, that in all cases of creation, a definite set of steps or stages is always involved and that this is the creative process. Wallas, and later Patrick, have proposed a description of these stages as follows: (i) preparation, during which the problem is investigated, (ii) incubation, during which one is not consciously thinking about the problem but unconscious mental processes are taking place, (iii) insight or illumination, during which the 'happy idea' occurs, and (iv) concretization or verification, during which the work achieves its final form.[18]

Such a division of what goes on during creation into distinct stages is artificial and misleading, however. What Patrick found was that the artists she studied tended first to try out a number of ideas; one idea would tend to recur; the artists would settle on an

## Product, Process, Person 77

idea and the creation would start to take shape; and finally they would elaborate on and revise the work. Such a process seems to describe a fairly ordinary procedure for organizing an activity, however, and does not really verify the existence of the distinctive stages which are described by Wallas and which are claimed to distinguish the creative process. Trying out a number of ideas and having one recur is quite different from Wallas's notion of incubation, which involves unconscious mental processes occurring during time away from an activity. And the settling on one idea after trying out a number does not capture the sense of the spontaneous generation of an idea which is central to the notion of insight or illumination. Indeed, Beardsley claims that the distinct stages of the creative process described by Wallas cannot really be distinguished in Patrick's material, and that:

> these activities are mixed together; they are constantly (or alternately) going on throughout the whole process.[19]

I likewise believe that it is not really possible to separate these various stages in actual acts of creation and that the process of creating must, therefore, be viewed as a whole. In terms of empirical investigations, there is very little evidence of a distinctive phase of incubation involving unconscious mental processes.[20] The oft quoted tales of Poincaré, who developed the theory of Fuchsian functions while stepping onto a bus and of Kekulé, who discovered the ring structure of benzene through a dream, seem to suggest that a period away from a problem is necessary in order for unconscious processes to do their work. Yet there is very little support for this in terms of actual research. Creators do not always take time away from their creative activities just prior to having an important idea. And even when such periods away from the problem are efficacious, there are a number of plausible explanations for this which do not involve unconscious processes, such as gaining rest or distance from the problem.[21]

Another problem with the stage account is that it is not always possible to identify an insight existing prior to concretization. A work of art may begin from any one of a number of different initial conditions, and some of these defy analysis in terms of prior insight and subsequent concretization. Khatchadourian has, in fact identified six different possible starting points for a work of art, ranging from a definite, well worked-out plan to hardly any advanced vision, and including, as well, a task or problem, the work of another artist, and certain conventional elements.[22] In some of these cases, particularly those in which there is very little advanced vision, it would be difficult to speak in terms of a prior insight which is subsequently concretized. An example would be the case of a dancer who puts on a record and then dances. He may have no pre-conceived idea to begin with, but may simply allow his body to move to the music. In such cases, we would not think of insight as existing prior to execution, but would consider insight to be present at various stages of the execution, or indeed, throughout the process. We might, in fact, think of the activity as being suffused with insight. Thus, it is difficult to separate insight from the actual making and view the latter in isolation. Similar cases are apparent in science. Watson's description of the process of discovering the structure of the DNA molecule creates a picture, not of a flash of insight followed by concretization, but rather of a lengthy and laborious process in which small insights played a role throughout.[23]

Moreover, it is difficult to delimit what precisely would constitute the phase of concretization. For example, does the making in poetry occur only when one has pen to paper? If a poem is composed in one's mind and never written down but only delivered orally, then what constitutes the concretization—the delivery? the working out of the poem in the mind? If the latter, then how can this be distinguished from insight? In cases such as these, one would likely refer to the whole process as creating. A similar difficulty seems evident with reference to scientific discovery. In the case of Kekulé's discovery of benzene rings through an insight gained through a dream, it is difficult to isolate a concretization phase. Although some verification may have been necessary, we would not equate the discovery with this verification as the insight was a significant factor in solving the problem. The entire process would constitute the discovery.

Perhaps, then, this model of prior insight and subsequent concretization might best yield to a more fluid conception of how insight and making are related. Collingwood, for example, sees art, not in terms of a pre-existing image which one then proceeds to execute, but rather in terms of a working out of what one wants to say in the process of execution.[24] Similarly, Howard sees artistic creation as involving constantly and mutually adjusting means and ends.[25] Finally, Maitland characterizes the process of creating art in terms of an interplay between what the artist brings to the work initially and the emerging work itself.[26] These views stress the idea that, in our terminology, insight exists as a part of the process of making.

It can be seen, then, that the aforementioned outline of stages is not an accurate description of how creating actually takes place. This type of artificial division of the process of creating into temporal stages does not do justice to the actual variety in creative activity. Furthermore, notions such as act of creation or moment of creation tend to give undue emphasis to one aspect of the process, namely insight, and so perhaps creating would be better understood in terms of creative activity which might take a variety of forms.

## *Persons*

A great deal of contemporary psychological testing and research has been directed toward attempting to determine what precisely are the characteristics of creative individuals and to identify such individuals in the general population.[27] The assumptions underlying such research are, first, that it is possible to identify individuals with some sort of creative potential or capacity, and second, that it is meaningful to talk about creative capacity, ability, or personality apart from consideration of products produced. Both these assumptions can be questioned.

Let us begin by looking at attempts to identify creative individuals in terms of cognitive abilities. Some of the abilities which have been suggested as characteristic of creative people include divergent thinking, ideational fluency, and flexibility. There are problems with such a characterization, however. First, there is no agreement amongst psychologists as to which cognitive abilities constitute creative capacity. There is disagreement, for example, as to the roles of convergent and divergent thinking.[28] There is no unequivocal evidence which links creativity clearly with a specific set of cognitive abilities. Moreover, our previous examination leads to the conclusion that such a link could not be found. The claim that certain specific cognitive abilities such as divergent thinking and ideational fluency characterize creativity is based on the view that creativity is marked by a specific process of thought. As demonstrated previously, however, this is not the case. Creating is not characterized entirely by divergent thinking, freely producing ideas, and suspending judgment, and Perkins has pointed out the fallacy of identifying creativity with ideational fluency.

The underlying problem with these psychological studies into creativity is that the findings of the tests have no demonstrable relationship to creating in real life. Generally, the method of proceeding is to postulate some abilities which are arrived at through an analysis of the notion of creativity, test for these abilities in order to divide individuals into groups, and then study the similarities and differences between the groups. The findings may, then, have some internal validity within the system, but they may have very little relationship to actual creating in real life.

One standard test item, for example, is to have the subject generate as many uses as possible for a common item such as a brick. The subject is then scored as to the number of uses generated and the novelty of the uses. Generating a large number of unusual uses is taken to be an indication of creativity. There is, however, no reason to believe that scoring highly on such a test is in any way an indication of creativity as defined by product. The ability to generate novel uses might be useful in some particular endeavour, but it is likely totally irrelevant to many creative activities. This type of skill would seem to have very little to do with the type of activity in which Dostoevsky or Einstein engaged, and we have no reason to expect that they would have scored highly on such tests. What the test is really testing is the ability to generate a large number of unusual responses, and the items are evaluated on the basis of their number and uniqueness, with no consideration of quality. Yet Dostoevsky's creativity lay not in generating a large number of unusual words, but rather in coming up with appropriate words in specific contexts and juxtaposing and combining words to create desired effects. His creativity was connected more with making aesthetic judgments and choices than with randomly generating novel responses. Similarly, Einstein was not engaged in simply generating as many unusual theories as he could, and then choosing among them. Rather, he was creative in coming up with a theory which solved a scientific problem. It is necessary, then, to distinguish between simply generating novel ideas and generating ideas which will solve a specific problem or meet a specific need. Skill at the former does not necessary entail skill at the latter, and this is a crucial difference which creativity tests ignore.

Psychologists themselves acknowledge that it is not clear what is actually being tested in tests of creativity. MacKinnon, for example, says of creativity tests that

> they fail to reveal the extent to which a person faced with a real life problem is likely to come up with solutions that are novel and adaptive and which he will be motivated to apply in all of their ramifications.[29]

In view of the difficulty of linking creativity with cognitive abilities, some investigators have focussed their research in the area of personality. They maintain that it is not cognitive ability which ultimately determines an individual's creativity, but one's personality traits, and some of the traits which are proposed as characterizing the creative personality are independence of mind, non-conformity, persistence, tolerance of ambiguity, and low sociability.[30] In addition, some researchers have found differences amongst artists and scientists in terms of personality. The artists tended to be non-conforming, amoral, and sensitive while the scientists tended to be assertive and unsociable.[31]

However, these characterizations of creative individuals are not universally valid. The model of the creative individual as a non-conforming, independent diverger has some notable exceptions. Copernicus, for example, was an extremely timid individual who bowed to authority, and Darwin was a patient, dogged collector of details. Neither fits the model of the creative individual proposed, and yet the fact that each was creative cannot be denied.

What such personality studies falsely assume is that all creative tasks are of a similar nature, and so there is one personality type who will be creative. This is not the case, however. Gardner has shown that there are, in fact, many human intellectual competences or intelligences which are relatively autonomous.[32] These include linguistic, musical, logical-mathematical, spatial, bodily-kinesthetic and personal intelligences. According to Gardner, the ability to operate with extreme effectiveness in one of these domains is relatively independent of high degrees of ability in other domains.

The nature of creative activities varies, then, with the specific discipline, the specific task, and the specific context and so will personality types. Copernicus, with his reverence for authority, may well have been precisely the type of person required to perform the synthesis which resulted in the Copernican system. Koestler says of him that:

> Only a conservative-minded person such as Copernicus could devote himself to the task of reconciling the irreconcilable doctrines of Aristotelian physics and Ptolemaic wheel-geometry on the one hand, with a sun-centred universe on the other.[33]

Similarly, Darwin's methodical nature likely aided him in making the painstaking compilation of data which led to his theory of evolution. And Newton claimed that his main advantage was the power of patient thought.

Now I do not wish to deny that there might be some traits of personality which might frequently be correlated to certain kinds of creative activity, nor that there are personality and motivational factors which affect whether and what an individual will create in specific circumstances. My objection, however, is to seeing such factors as defining creativity and as the basis for attempting to distinguish creative from non-creative individuals. There may be reasons why artists and scientists tend to display certain personality traits which have little to do with being creative *per se* but have more to do with how the discipline is carried on in a culture at a specific time. For example, scientists who are engaged in a type of scientific activity which involves long periods of isolated work in a laboratory may well test as unsociable. And innovative artists working during a period where there is reverence for tradition and no support for innovation may need to be independent-minded in order to achieve. But it would be as much an error to see these traits as defining the creative individual as it would be to conclude from the fact that most eminent scientists today are male that being male is a necessary condition for being a creative scientist. A further danger is that such traits and abilities will be used as criteria of exclusion, so that some individuals may be denied opportunities on the grounds that they do not exhibit a 'creative' personality.

There is a basic problem underlying all the difficulties which beset attempts to define creativity as it relates to people, and that is the problematic nature of the notion of creative capacity or potential. J.P. White, in his reply to Parsons,[34] demonstrates some of the difficulties in attempting to understand what precisely this could mean. There are, he points out, a variety of ways in which one may be said to have a capacity and each way is tied to a specific context. For example, a baby may be said to have the capacity to produce valuable work in a way in which inanimate objects do not, but an art student has such a capacity in a way in which the baby does not. But neither may actually produce anything of value. Parsons seems to have something more in mind than creative capacity in either of these senses, however. White states, further, that creative capacity might be understood in the sense of actually having produced something of value, but this interpretation renders the notion of capacity ineffectual. Moreover, this could not have been Parsons's intention, as he claims that one can be creative without ever having produced anything.

White ends his analysis in bewilderment, but let us explore this problem further. We might compare the use of capacity in the context of creativity with another use which is more easily understood. We say of a factory that it has a certain productive capacity. We seem to mean by this something like the following: all the necessary elements are in place so that, when set in motion, all things being equal, the factory will produce x. In this case it is fairly easy to specify what are the necessary elements, for example the equipment, the materials, the manpower, and also those factors which might be included under 'all things being equal', for example absence of strikes, fire, or bankruptcy of the supplier. One cannot specify the conditions in this way for creative capacity, however, since the factors involved are so numerous, so complex, and so variable. Whether people actually create and what they create is affected by their abilities, how well they think and work in the discipline in question, by their skills, talents, imagination, personality, style, and values, as well as by the state of the discipline, and the context in which they work (for example, mentors, associates, the working environment, the values of the society, support both financial and psychological, chance occurrences).[35]

One might argue that creative capacity refers to those factors mentioned above which relate directly to the individual such as abilities, talent, and personality, and that a person with the proper combination of factors would, given the appropriate environmental circumstances, create. The difficulty with this view, however, is that an individual does not simply act within an environment, but rather interacts with it, and so one cannot really separate the personal from the environmental factors. Individuals will react differently in various circumstances and it would be exceedingly difficult, perhaps even impossible, to try to specify the exact context within which each individual would be likely to create.[36] Thus it is difficult to see how the notion of creative capacity can be meaningful in terms of providing any real indication of the likelihood of a person creating.

The notion of creativity is sometimes linked to persons in another sense that bears examination. This is the notion embodied in the view that education should foster an individual's creativity, taken in the sense of personal growth. Here creativity is not related to the production of valuable products, since one of the principal ideas of this theory is that it is the process and not the product which is important for creativity. Furthermore, it is claimed that it might be more beneficial for a person's creativity to create an inferior product. What, then, can be meant by this notion of creativity? It seems to me that 'creativity' is used here as a broad, general term whose meaning varies according to the context and that it is used instead of some other, more precise term such as problem-solving abilities, self-expression, self-confidence, originality, spontaneity, divergence, flexibility, adaptability, non-authoritarian learning, and mental health. The conflation of these two types of uses is based on the assumption that creativity involves a specific process, and that this process is characterized by some or all of these qualities. Our previous analysis has, I believe, demonstrated the fallacy of the former assumption. Thus there are no grounds for linking creating necessarily with any of the aforementioned outcomes. It is a contingent matter whether a person who creates will be more flexible or confident, and there are ample counter-examples to the connection alleged between creating and mental health, Van Gogh to name but one.

## *Summary*

In this chapter, the focus on process and person which characterizes the common view of creativity has been challenged. It has been argued that there is not a distinctive creative process which is different from ordinary thought processes, but that the process of creating just is the process of excellent thinking and performing in an area.

The idea that we can meaningfully speak of a creative person in a sense other than referring to a person who actually creates has likewise been shown to be mistaken. This common view of creative person rests on the notion of a distinctive creative process at which some people excel, and thus falls with the demise of the process account.

The conclusion we are left with is that creativity entails creating; it refers to the actual creation of products which are significant in a particular context. Creativity is not, then, highly mysterious, irrational or unique, but involves, rather, the excellent use of our ordinary processes of thinking in so far as they issue in outstanding products. Creativity is achieving extraordinary ends.

## NOTES

1. J.P. White, "Creativity and Education: A Philosophical Analysis," *British Journal of Educational Studies* 16 (1968): 123-137; M.J. Parsons, "White and Black and Creativity," *British Journal of Educational Studies* 19 (1971): 5-16.
2. White, "Creativity and Education," p.126.
3. Arthur Koestler, *The Act of Creation* (New York: MacMillan, 1964).
4. De Bono, *Lateral Thinking*.
5. See for example, Vincent Tomas, "Creativity in Art," in W.E. Kennick, ed., *Art and Philosophy* (New York: St. Martin's Press 1964), pp. 283-294.
6. Vernon Howard, *Artistry: The Work of Artists* (Indianapolis: Hackett Publishing Company, 1982), pp. 110ff.
7. Ibid., p. 120.
8. H. Poincaré, *The Foundations of Science*, in P.E. Vernon, ed., *Creativity*, p.80.
9. This example was used by De Bono at a workshop at the University of Toronto on November 10, 1979 entitled "Teaching Thinking."
10. R.G. Collingwood, *The Principles of Art* (London: Oxford University Press, 1974), pp.28-29.
11. In David Perkins, *The Mind's Best Work* (Cambridge: Harvard University Press, 1981), pp.67-68.
12. Perkins, *Mind's Best Work*, p.279.
13. Richard Paul, "Critical Thinking and the Critical Person," in J. Bishop, J. Lochhead, and D.N. Perkins, eds. *Teaching: Progress in Research and Teaching* (Hillsdale, N.J.: Erlbaum, 1987).
14. See Stillman Drake, *Galileo at Work* (Chicago: The University of Chicago Press, 1978).
15. Jerome Bruner, *Beyond the Information Given* (New York: Norton, 1973).
16. David Weisberg, *Creativity: Genius and Other Myths* (New York: W.H. Freeman and Company, 1986).

17. Perkins, *Mind's Best Work*.
18. Graham Wallas, *The Art of Thought* (New York: Harcourt, Brace, 1926); Catharine Patrick, "Creative Thought in Artists," *Journal of Psychology* 4 (1937): 35-73.
19. Monroe Beardsley, "On the Creation of Art," in L.A. Jacobus, ed., *Aesthetics and the Arts* (New York: McGraw Hill, 1968), pp.53-72.
20. Weisberg, *Creativity*, pp.19-34; Perkins, *Mind's Best Work*, pp.50-57.
21. Ibid.
22. Haig Khatchadourian,"The Creative Process in Art," *British Journal of Aesthetics* 17 (1977): 230-241.
23. James Watson, *The Double Helix* (New York: Mentor Books, 1968).
24. Collingwood, *Principles of Art*, pp.28-29.
25. Howard, *Artistry*, Chapter 5.
26. Jeffrey Maitland, "Creativity," *Journal of Aesthetics and Art Criticism* 34 (Summer 1976): 407.
27. See, for example, J. Freeman, *Creativity: A Selective Review of Research*, 2nd edition (London: Society for Research into Higher Education, 1971).
28. See, for example, J.W. Getzels and P.W. Jackson, *Creativity and Intelligence* (New York: John Wiley and Sons, 1962); Liam Hudson, *Contrary Imaginations* (Baltimore: Penguin Books, 1966).
29. D.W. MacKinnon, "Education for Creativity: A Modern Myth?" in J. Freeman, *Creativity*, p.26; Cf. A.J. Butcher who states that there has not been satisfactory evidence to support the assumption that "high ability on tests of divergent thinking is evidence of creativeness in real life as evidenced by eg. scientific or artistic achievement."; "Divergent Thinking and Creativity," in J. Freeman, *Creativity*, p.87; See also R.J. Shapiro's discussion in "Creative research scientists," *Psychologia Africana, Monograph Supplement* 4 (1968): 37-45.
30. See, for example, Barron, *Creativity and Psychological Health*; D.W. MacKinnon, "Study of American Architects."
31. See, for example, Anne Roe, *The Making of a Scientist* (New York: Dodd, Mead, 1952); F. Barron, *Artists in the Making* (New York: Seminar Press, 1972).
32. Howard Gardner, *Frames of Mind: The Theory of Multiple Intelligences* (New York: Basic Books, Inc., 1983).
33. Arthur Koestler, *The Sleepwalkers* (London: Hutchinson, 1959), p.214.
34. White, note to Parsons, "White and Black and Creativity."
35. One good example of the interaction of all these factors in an actual case of scientific discovery is Gerald Holton's description of the work of Fermi. *The Scientific Imagination* (New York: Cambridge University Press, 1978).
36. Howard Gardner proposes a research program to illuminate creativity which would take into consideration this range of factors. Whether such research could issue in a theory able not only to explain instances of creativity *post facto*, but also to predict future creativity is very much an open question. "Freud in Three Frames: A Cognitive-Scientific Approach to Creativity," *Daedalus* 115, 3, (1986).

# Chapter IV

# RULES, SKILLS, AND KNOWLEDGE

ONE CENTRAL tenet of the contemporary view is that creativity necessarily involves going beyond or breaking rules, and that this is, in fact, its defining characteristic. This idea is based on the view, examined previously, that ordinary thinking is confined within rigid frameworks. These frameworks are characterized by rules which define the modes of proceeding within the framework, but they cannot provide the means to transcend the framework itself. Such rules are, in fact, seen to be inhibiting to creativity because they tend to keep one locked into the prevailing framework.

This view is manifested in several different forms depending on the context and the type of rule involved. One common form of the view, a version which is frequently applied to the arts, is that internalized rules or skills are inhibiting to creativity because they confine one to habitual and mechanized modes of operation. Koestler offers a summary of this point of view:

> Matrices vary from fully automatized skills to those with a high degree of plasticity; but even the latter are controlled by rules of the game which function below the level of awareness. These silent codes can be regarded as condensations of learning into habit. Habits are the indispensable core of stability and ordered behaviour; they also have a tendency to become mechanized and to reduce man to the status of a conditioned automaton. The creative act, by connecting previously unrelated dimensions of experience, enables him to attain to a higher level of mental evolution. It is an act of liberation—the defeat of habit by originality.[1]

Another version of the view that rules are inhibiting to creativity centres on rules of method and is applied most often with respect to science. Here the argument is that there is no one fixed method which characterizes all of scientific practice, and that discovery is only possible through the breaking of existing rules of method. This is the view expressed by Feyerabend:

> We find then, that there is not a single rule, however plausible, and however firmly grounded in epistemology, that is not violated at some time or other. It becomes evident that such violations are not accidental events, they are not the results of insufficient knowledge or of inattention which might be avoided. On the contrary, we see that they are necessary for progress.[2]

The principal assumption which underlies all these views regarding the constraining force of rules, skills, and knowledge is succinctly expressed in the following statement by De Bono:

> Too much experience within a field may restrict creativity because you know so well how things *should be done* that you are unable to escape to come up with new ideas.[3]

The central task of this chapter will be to challenge the view that rules, skills and knowledge are inhibiting to creativity. It will be argued that this view rests on a misunderstanding of the nature of the various types of rules and of their role in creative endeavours, and furthermore that such rules are crucial to and, in fact, enhance the possibility of creative achievement.

## *Rules and Art*

The first question to be addressed is whether artistic creativity does indeed necessarily involve going beyond or breaking rules. This rule-breaking model is certainly not an accurate characterization of all creative activity in the arts. Most artistic work is not revolutionary, but rather takes place within the confines of a framework and is characterized by adherence to the rules dictated by a tradition, a school, a style, or a genre. The painter is directed by the rules of style and technique of the relevant school of painting. The poet is subject to the traditional limitations of form and language. The dancer's work is limited by the forms and conventions of the particular style of dance. A classical ballet dancer, for example, will abide by the principles of classical ballet and try to master the techniques which are consequent to them. A poet composing a sonnet is constrained by the sonnet form and must produce a poem with fourteen lines, a specified metre, rhyme scheme, mood, division of ideas, and so on, in order for it to be evaluated as a successful sonnet. Indeed, one may contend that the genius of many outstanding artists lies not so much in their innovative departures, but rather in the excellence of their achievements within the limits set by these rules.

It is true, however, that not all artistic endeavour takes place within the confines of strict adherence to a framework. Art develops and changes by the creation of novel works which depart from existing frameworks, and some rules of the framework are broken or repudiated in the process. This may involve the rejection of explicitly formulated doctrines or the unearthing of presuppositions which had been implicit, the recognition of them as conventions, and thus their rejection. An example of the first type might be the rejection on the part of many modern poets of some conventions of form such as traditional metre, rhyme, stanza form, punctuation, or capitalization. An example of the latter would be the recognition by absurdist dramatists of realism as a convention in theatre, and its subsequent rejection in favour of other possibilities. Thus the very existence of works of art which depart from the rules of a framework and which, at least temporarily, are not completely subsumed under any existing framework demonstrates one way in which artistic creation is not totally determined by these sorts of rules. Artistic creation can involve breaking or going beyond rules.

Even in such cases, however, not all rules are broken, as we have already seen. Indeed, an innovation is meaningful only because the innovator continues to operate within the context of rules which are substantially unchanged. Artistic creation, even of a revolutionary sort, is usually less radical a departure from the existing framework than we tend to believe. The rule-breaking model underestimates the importance of adherence to the rules of specific frameworks in creative enterprises.

One important way in which artistic activity can be seen to be rule-governed is in terms of the rules of the particular artistic domain which are internalized and become skills which govern thought and performance. Do such skills inhibit creativity?

There is a long-standing debate concerning this issue which harks back at least to the Greeks. On the one side, there is the view that the essence of art is inspiration, and that artists do not really understand what they are doing or how they do it. Artistic creation is seen as essentially irrational. Plato, for example, has Socrates say in the *Ion* that:

> all the good poets who make epic poems use no art at all, but they are inspired and possessed when they utter all these beautiful poems... Not by art, then, they make their poetry, but by divine dispensation.[4]

The opposed view sees art mainly in terms of the perfection of skills and the essence of art as technique. 'Techne' is, in fact, a central concept for Aristotle's theory of art, which he views as 'a productive state that is truly reasoned'.[5] The skills, the technique, the 'art' (in Plato's sense) involved are part of what we generally think of as craft, and so this issue of the role of skills in art is connected with the nature of the distinction between art and craft and the role of the latter in the former. The two views presented exemplify opposing positions concerning this relationship. The view of divine inspiration excludes craft from the realm of art while the techne view reduces art to craft.

The reluctance of some contemporary theorists to admit skill into the realm of creativity appears to be connected with this Platonic vision of the act of creation as mysterious, inexplicable, and unanticipated. This can be demonstrated by looking at Collingwood's characterization of art and craft. Collingwood draws a sharp distinction between the two, and sees the essence of art as lying in the way in which it is different from craft. The main characteristics of craft which he outlines are that it involves: 1) a means - end relationship, 2) a distinction between planning and execution, 3) a progression from raw material to finished product, and 4) an imposition of form upon matter. Art, on the other hand, cannot display any of these characteristics. It does not involve, on the part of the artist, a pre-existing goal or idea which is then consciously worked toward by means of the medium, transforming some raw material into a finished work by imposing a form on some pre-existing matter. For Collingwood, the essence of art lies in the fact that the end does not really exist until the work is completed. It involves, essentially, the expression of emotions and this is achieved only in the course of the execution of a work. If this is the case, then the essence of art cannot lie in the perfection of technique. Making something purely technically is a feature of craft and implies a preconceived end, but Collingwood states that in art:

> the end is not something foreseen and preconceived to which appropriate means can be thought out in the light of

our knowledge of its special character. Expression is an activity of which there can be no technique.[6]

This sort of claim about the impossibility of foreknowledge is made frequently in art theory,[7] and has something in common with the divine inspiration view. The main point is that creativity necessarily involves spontaneity, imagination, and the generation of novelty but that these are a logical impossibility if the end is conceived beforehand. Thus the creative process retains an element of the unexpected, the unforeseen, the mysterious.

The basic problem with such a view, however, is that it becomes difficult, if not impossible, to explain how the artist exercises control in creating the work of art.[8] Howard describes this as the creativity paradox:

> that the artist both knows and does not know what he is up to, that he directs without foresight or preconception.[9]

There have been some attempts to explain how control is possible given this account, but they are, on the whole, unsatisfactory. Collingwood himself asserts that art involves the expression of an emotion, and that the artist does not know what this emotion is until it has been expressed by creating the work of art. Thus the emotion is discovered and clarified in the course of executing the work, and therein lies the element of control. The weaknesses of Collingwood's view have been pointed out frequently.[10] Although creating a work of art may sometimes involve, for the artist, a process of discovering emotions, there seems no reason to believe that this need always be the case. The artist's emotions may be relatively clear at the outset and may not have to be discovered. In addition, emotions may simply be irrelevant to the creation of some works. Tomas's view of control as manifested by inspiration 'kicking' the artist through inner twinges is similarly plagued with difficulties.[11] It does not go very far towards explaining the critical nature of the control and ignores the goals in light of which judgments are made.

The failure of these 'Unforeseen' theories points to the conclusion that the question of foreknowledge is really a spurious issue. There is a considerable variety of starting points from which an artist may begin a work of art, and no one of them is privileged. An artist may, for example, begin a painting with a clear idea of the desired effect—to convey the expression in the eyes of a certain individual or the impression of a particular scene; the artist may begin, however, with only a vague and inarticulate feeling; or a painting may be initiated without any pre-existing image, but simply out of a desire to experiment with certain combinations of colours and textures, or with certain techniques until an aesthetically pleasing result is achieved. There is no good reason to deny the status of art to any work because of its mode of inception.

That there can be this range of starting points for works of art indicates that the creative process cannot be characterized in terms of a necessary lack of foreknowledge. The control which is exercised in the process of creating a work of art is a product of a variety of factors including what the artist knows at the beginning as well as the state of the work of art at any given moment. Maitland describes this relationship, saying:

> each artist must bring to the creative enterprise an entire background of habits, theories, habitualized techniques, methods, and ideas for what he wants to achieve. As he works, some of these forehavings will determine certain choices, and as the work emerges some of these forehavings may have to be modified or given up entirely. In any case, the work of art grows from the artist's dialogue with himself and his forehavings on the one hand and the emerging work of art and its demands on the other.[12]

Where does this discussion leave us with respect to our initial question about the role of skills and of craft in art? It has been demonstrated that there is little support for a view which would exclude craft from art. There is critical control maintained in the production of a work of art, and skills are involved in exercising this type of judgment. The question remains as to whether skills might still be inhibiting to innovation.

We come, then, to a second main assumption which underlies the view that skills and rules are necessarily inhibiting to creativity, the assumption that skills are simply habits. This assumption is based on the idea that skills, once learned, become automatic, operating below the level of consciousness, and fixing predetermined ways of seeing and behaving. Once in the grip of these unconscious constraints, it is thought that we are no longer aware that they operate nor that our action is rule-bound; thus it becomes extremely difficult, if not impossible, to go beyond the rules and to innovate. Koestler expresses this point of view:

> The force of habit, the grip of convention, hold us down on the Trivial Plane; we are unaware of our bondage because the bonds are invisible, their restraints acting below the level of awareness. They are the collective standards of value, codes of behaviour, matrices with built in axioms which determine the rules of the game, and make most of us run, most of the time, in the grooves of habit—reducing us to the status of skilled automata which Behaviourism proclaims to be the only condition of man.[13]

In views such as this, skills are seen as identical with habits—as rigid, unthinking, and inflexible. Indeed, William James saw such habits as pervading all our behaviour and constituting the mainstay of our activity.

> Habit is thus a second nature...- at any rate as regards its importance in adult life; for the acquired habits of our training have by that time inhibited or strangled most of the natural impulsive tendencies which were originally there. Ninety-nine hundredths or, possibly, nine hundred and ninety-nine thousandths of our activity is purely automatic and habitual[14]

This portrayal of skills as habits is not accurate, however. A number of philosophers, including Ryle, Scheffler, and Howard, have taken great care to point out how skills and habits differ. If a habit involves the performance of an action blindly, without thought, a true skill can be seen to involve just the opposite. Ryle, for example, states:

> When we describe someone as doing something by pure or blind habit, we mean that he does it automatically and without having to mind what he is doing. He does not exercise care, vigilance, or criticism.[15]

For Ryle, however, care, vigilance, and criticism must be involved in a skill.

> A person's performance is described as careful or skilful if in his operations he is ready to detect and correct lapses, to repeat and improve upon successes, to profit from the examples of others and so forth.[16]

The main point here is that, in terming an action skilled, we are emphasizing just this critical, careful aspect. A skilled performance is one which is not purely automatic and totally inflexible, but is able to adjust to changing circumstances. A habit is acquired deliberately or inadvertently by continual repetition of an action, and may be either desirable or undesirable—there are good and bad habits. In the case of skill, however, one deliberately sets out to learn, and it is acquired, not through mere repetition, but through training. One can continually improve upon a skill and eventually attain mastery and hence freedom in the sense that what one wants to do one can do. The notions of proficiency or mastery do not apply to habits.

There are, of course, certain habitual elements which constitute a part of most skills. The ability to spell for writing or manual dexterity with scales for playing the piano would be examples. But there is more involved in a skill than such routine and automatic facilities. A skill also involves judgment. It involves applying the ability in a variety of circumstances and making changes when appropriate. A painter is skilful not only in terms of the brush strokes he employs, but also in how he uses them in a specific work—how he makes adjustments according to the way the work is progressing. A pianist's skill goes beyond her technical proficiency at the keyboard to involve, as well, her judgments as to tempo or volume.

The distinction between habit and skill is parallelled to some extent by that between drill and training. Drill involves continual repetition and what is inculcated by drill will be a habit. A skill, on the other hand, is learned through training which may contain some elements of drill, but will involve more than this. Training involves the development of critical skill and must involve some degree of understanding. Scheffler provides an account of skill development which emphasizes this distinction, as follows:

> critical skills call for strategic judgment and cannot be rendered automatic. To construe the learning of chess as a matter of drill would thus be quite wrong-headed in suggesting that the same game be played over and over again, or intimating that going through the motions of playing repeatedly somehow improves one's game. What is rather supposed, at least in the case of chess, is that improvement comes about through development of strategic judgment, which requires that such judgment be allowed

opportunity to guide choices in a wide variety of games, with maximal opportunity for evaluating relevant outcomes and reflecting upon alternative principles and strategy in the light of such evaluation.[17]

Howard goes even farther than this to contend that even drill cannot be construed as mere mindless repetition. He argues that practice of any sort involves an effort to improve according to some standard, and thus some thought and judgment. Of the practice of advanced musicians, for example, he states:

> Rather than mechanically duplicating a passage, one strives for particular goals, say, of fluency, contrast, or balance. Successive repeats reflect a drive toward such goals rather than passive absorption of a sequence of motor acts.[18]

The reason skills have been assimilated with habits by some theorists seems to be related to the fact that skills, like habits, frequently operate below the level of awareness. This being so, it is assumed that the element of control cannot be present and that skills must be blind and thoughtless. This certainly need not be the case, however. There are many skills which are routine and of which we are not consciously aware, but over which we still exercise control. The skill of driving a car is a good example. Although an experienced driver is not conscious of the skills used in manipulating the vehicle through traffic, nonetheless full control is maintained. The driver makes adjustments according to the changing traffic conditions and is, in fact, in control because of and not despite these skills. Thus the lack of explicit awareness does not seem to preclude the possibility of control.

The skills which are manifested in the arts certainly seem to be examples of this type of implicit knowledge. As an artist becomes more and more skilled, it is not only technical expertise, but also judgment which becomes assimilated into physical responses, and so, as Gilson says:

> Man does not think *with* his hands, but the intellect of a painter certainly thinks *in* his hands, so much so that, in moments of manual inspiration, an artist can sometimes let the hand do its job without bothering too much about what it does.[19]

This does not imply that such skills, which operate to some extent below the level of awareness, are automatic and lacking in judgment, but rather that some judgments can be executed without conscious attention. They are, however, still judgments. Critical skills cannot, however, be totally reduced to routine performances, for they involve making choices according to changing circumstances.

Nonetheless, some aspects of critical skills can be improved with practice, and one can reach the stage where one can accomplish them with speed, accuracy, finesse — and seeming effortlessness. This is part of what is involved in doing something well. The proficiency in certain more fundamental aspects of a skill is what allows one to achieve higher levels. The mastery of a certain level of skill is what allows one to go on, and the possibilities for further development seem unlimited. Thus new ground is broken in a field by critical judgment, but this judgment is itself based upon a repertoire of acquired and assimilated skills in the discipline.

It is now time to return to the question with which we began, the question of whether rules are inhibiting to creativity. We have seen that the acquisition of certain types of skills is often connected with a high level of achievement in a discipline. Nonetheless it might still be asked whether skills might not, at times, inhibit creativity by fixing a pre-determined way of seeing and operating, and thus limiting the possibilities for innovation. It could be pointed out that even those with a great deal of technical proficiency in an area can and sometimes do perform in a mechanized, unthinking manner. What, then, is the difference between instances where skills manifest creativity and those where they do not? Moreover, it might be claimed that there is a difference between doing something well according to certain rules and going beyond or changing those rules, and that the acquisition of skills is an aid only to the former, but is, in fact, a hindrance to the latter.

The response to these questions has, I believe, been indicated in the course of the previous and present chapters. With reference to the latter issue, it has been shown that there is not a real discontinuity between achieving highly within the rules of a discipline and achieving highly when it entails going beyond or changing some rules. The latter is, rather, an extension of the former. It would be incorrect to view any discipline or creative activity as taking place within rigid boundaries and being totally delimited and defined by rules. Instead, the possibilities for what can be achieved are really open-ended. Furthermore, one never breaks all the rules, since to do so would be to abandon the discipline. And when rules are broken in the course of significant achievement, it is generally by a master of the discipline who is at such an advanced stage in the discipline that he can see the point in doing so. It seems, then, that one difference between creative and uncreative performances relates to having a real understanding of the discipline in which one is engaged. If, for example, a musician were technically proficient but nonetheless played mechanically, we might suspect that she does not really understand music. The skills in question would be of a rather limited sort, encompassing only technical expertise but not highly developed judgment. If, however, an artist is highly skilled and at the cutting edge of the discipline and has a real understanding of the discipline, then he is in a position to go beyond or change rules if this seems necessary.

Now it is possible that the manner in which skills are taught and learned might make a difference to the creativeness of the outcome. Skills are not mere habits but involve critical judgments applied in a variety of changing circumstances. Thus the teaching of skills as flexible abilities related to ends which may vary might obviate the possibility of rigidity and mechanization. In addition, skills must be understood within the broader context of the discipline as a whole. It is important to develop the ability to see beyond the specific problem or issue with which one is dealing and to have a real understanding of the methods and procedures of the discipline and the principles and goals which lie behind them.

In summary, then, it seems clear that learning skills is important for creativity. This is in contrast to the view that skills are mere habits which lock one into an established way of seeing and prevent one from going beyond the rules. First, it seems to be the case that some pure habits are necessary and vital for creating. Habits such as accurate spelling or manual dexterity at the keyboard are the foundation for more complex skills, and no high level creativity would be possible without them. The second point is that many skills are not reducible to habits, but involve critical judgment and adjustment to changing circumstances. Thus they do not lock one into one way of seeing and are not incompatible with the possibility of changing rules, if necessary. I would further want to claim that one is, in fact, more likely to be in a position to go beyond or change rules, to make a breakthrough and advance a discipline if one is working at an extremely highly skilled level at the cutting edge of the discipline.

## Rules and Science

The notion that rules are inhibiting to creativity has not been confined to the arts, but has been applied to science as well. Here the argument which is made closely parallels the one offered with respect to the arts, namely that the rules which underlie any scientific activity are specific to the particular framework but cannot be of assistance when what is required is the transcending of the framework itself. This is precisely what is required in the case of revolutionary scientific discovery, however, and so rules are constraining to innovation in science.

We can begin by asking in which sense the notion of rules can be applied to science. One possibility would be in terms of the kinds of skills which we looked at in the field of artistic creation. The sort of internalized rule which results in skilled performance does not seem to be applicable in science in quite the same way as in the arts, however. Although there is some skilful manipulation of instrumentation involved in the practice of science, it is not essentially a performance activity relying heavily on internalized physical responses the way singing or even painting are. Nonetheless the skills of judgment are certainly involved in scientific activity, and it is with respect to such judgment that one form of the 'rules as inhibiting' argument is deployed. It is argued that judgments can only be made with reference to the rules of a particular framework, but that discovery necessarily involves changing frameworks and so too the rules of the framework. Thus the rules of one framework cannot lead to discovery. Michael Polanyi makes the point as follows:

> Major discoveries change our interpretative framework. Hence it is logically impossible to arrive at these by the continued application of our previous interpretative framework.[20]

Instead of rules, then, flexibility and open-mindedness are considered the cornerstones of discovery. The effective scientist must, it is believed:

> lack prejudice to a degree where he can look at the most 'self-evident' facts or concepts without necessarily accepting them, and, conversely, allow his imagination to play with the most unlikely possibilities.[21]

This sort of argument is given support by views such as Kuhn's which emphasize the revolutionary nature of discovery in science. To recap the essential elements of the Kuhnian view which are relevant here, Kuhn sees scientific discovery as involving a paradigm shift or radical change in the perspective from which we view scientific phenomena, categorize data, and organize research. Between revolutions there are periods of normal science in which the implications of the new theory are worked out. Furthermore, the paradigms which succeed one another in the course of scientific development are seen to be irreconcilable, and so it is discontinuity in scientific development which is stressed. If this picture is accurate and scientific development does exhibit this sort of discontinuity, then the rules of one framework would be inapplicable in terms of making discoveries.

The problematic nature of Kuhn's view and its radical dichotomy between revolutionary and normal science has been pointed out previously. It is much too rigid and does not do justice to the continuity which is evident in scientific development. Not everything changes in the face of a discovery. There must be some common elements in light of which the changed elements are meaningful. If this is the case, then the prevailing framework or conceptual scheme and its accompanying rules are important for scientific discovery.

Kuhn himself acknowledges that normal scientific practice, with its emphasis on the rules of a specific framework, is essential to the progress of science, and that discoveries would not be possible without it. He goes so far, in fact, as to state that too much emphasis has been placed upon divergent thinking and flexibility in psychological accounts of scientific creativity, and that science would not have exhibited the progress which it has if scientists were not oriented exclusively in a unique tradition. He says:

> only investigations firmly rooted in the contemporary scientific tradition are likely to break that tradition and give rise to a new one.[22]

And later he states:

> I hope to have made meaningful the view that the productive scientist must be a traditionalist who enjoys playing intricate games by pre-established rules in order to be a successful innovator who discovers new rules and new pieces with which to apply them.[23]

As was the case for artistic creation, so also in scientific activity, it is those who are most highly skilled and knowledgeable within a specific tradition who will be in the best position to make changes in that tradition.

Another version of the view that rules are inhibiting to scientific discovery is in terms of rules of method. The traditional picture of science involves the idea that the scientific enterprise is characterized by a very specific method, the scientific method, and that adherence to this method is what gives scientific knowledge its special status and what enables science to progress. Many recent theorists have called this view into question, however, claiming that there are no rules of method which are consistent and invariable with respect to all scientific practice. Moreover, some even maintain that such rules of method would be detrimental to scientific discovery and progress.

The latter is the view held by Feyerabend, who denies that there is such a thing as a scientific method in actual scientific practice, and furthermore asserts that progress would be impossible if there were. He says:

> The idea of a method that contains firm, unchanging and absolutely binding principles for conducting the business of science meets considerable difficulty when confronted with the results of historical research....Indeed, one of the most striking features of recent discussions in the history and philosophy of science is the realization that events and developments, such as the invention of atomism in antiquity, the Copernican Revolution, the rise of modern atomism, the gradual emergence of the wave theory of light, occurred only because some thinkers either *decided* not to be bound by certain 'obvious' methodological rules, or because they *unwittingly broke* them.[24]

His denial of the existence of a unique scientific method is based on an examination of historical instances. Feyerabend claims that none of the methodological rules which are commonly proposed as characterizations of the scientific method are consistently adhered to in actual practice. He argues that scientists do not, in fact, abandon theories on the basis of contradictory evidence, but use falsified theories all the time, saving them by means of questioning the testing methods or the auxiliary hypotheses. Anomalies do not, then, cause a theory's abandonment, as some proponents of scientific method would claim, since all theories

## Rules, Skills, and Knowledge 101

contain, and indeed must contain, anomalies. Science then, according to Feyerabend, often proceeds counter-inductively, using hypotheses that are in opposition to established theories or facts.

The claim is not, however, that scientists ought to use good scientific method but are remiss in actual practice. It is rather that the existence of such a method, of such rigid rules of procedure, would actually inhibit scientific progress. Feyerabend's argument for this proceeds as follows. There are metaphysical presuppositions (what he calls natural interpretations) inherent in every theory. They are:

> ideas so closely connected with observations that it needs a special effort to realize their existence and to determine their content.[25]

These natural interpretations are closely related to sensory impressions and are embedded in observation language. Thus a prevailing theory will determine the way in which experience is seen and described and so will never be refuted by observation or analysis. It is, then, self-perpetuating. The only way the hold of a prevailing theory can be broken and progress can be made is by the positing of an entirely new theory, unconnected with the old one, with its own new natural interpretations. The old theory can then be analysed in the light of the new theory. This sort of activity, however, does not and indeed could not conform to a method since any rules of method would keep one locked into the prevailing theory. It is, rather, irrational and anarchistic. The only method which Feyerabend acknowledges as applicable to scientific discovery is 'anything goes'.

Feyerabend's view is another version of the argument which we have met before which states that rules are necessarily inhibiting to creativity because they keep one locked into a specific framework. And as a version of this argument, it is subject to the same problems. It presupposes that frameworks are fixed, rigid, and unconnected, but the discussion in Chapter III has demonstrated the untenability of this view of frameworks. Moreover, the demonstration in Chapters I and II of continuities between successive theories further undercuts Feyerabend's argument regarding the incommensurability of theories and the consequent necessity of ignoring all rules and positing entirely new theories in an unconstrained manner.

In order to further assess this issue of scientific method, it is necessary to differentiate two senses in which the claim regarding the impossibility of scientific method can be made. One is the view that there is no scientific method in terms of definitive rules for the evaluation of scientific theories. This is a view which was examined in detail in Chapter II and refuted. It was argued that not all rules are broken in the case of a discovery and that the rules that are continuous between theories provide one basis for the assessment of new theories. Another basis is provided by the overarching methodological meta-criteria which transcend particular frameworks. Although it does seem to be the case that there is no one procedure or technique for assessment which can be seen as *the* method of science, scientific method can be appropriately construed in terms of its general principles of appraisal.[26]

The second sense in which claims are made regarding the impossibility of scientific method is with respect to rules for the generation or creation of scientific hypotheses or theories. Some philosophers such as Feyerabend would deny that there can be a method of science with respect to either the generation or the evaluation of theories, and would, in fact, deny the distinction between the two. For others, however, this distinction is crucial.[27] Popper, for example, fully endorses the notion that there is a scientific method in terms of a method for the assessment of theories but sees the generation of theories as an irrational process which admits of no logical method.[28]

Now it must be granted that there is no logic of discovery in terms of an algorithmic procedure for creating scientific hypotheses or theories. There are no specific procedures which will ensure the generation of successful theories. In this Bacon was mistaken and Popper is correct. Nonetheless, this does not imply that scientific discovery is irrational and not at all rule-governed. On the contrary, the process of discovery is very much constrained by rules. Even in cases of the creation of radically new theories where some methodological rules are broken, most rules are followed. And even the violation of specific rules is ultimately governed by the kinds of methodological meta-rules which constrain the assessment of theories. In scientific discovery, rules are violated in order to solve an outstanding problem, and the meta-rules which govern the ultimate appraisal of the proposed solution such as fit with data, simplicity, and fruitfulness exercise control over the possibilities which are generated. Thus the criteria of justification and the methodological meta-rules which issue from them play a central role in discovery as well.

One reason for the general failure to acknowledge the crucial role of rules in discovery as well as in evaluation might be related to the separation made between discovery and justification. Now this distinction is certainly an important one in philosophy of science and is absolutely necessary in order to properly locate scientific rationality in justificatory principles and to eliminate psychological and sociological factors from the epistemological endeavour.[29] It is an error, however, to conceive of actual scientific activity as neatly separable into a generative phase which is non-evaluative and a subsequent evaluative phase. It is one thing to make a conceptual distinction between discovery and justification in order to rule out psychological factors from consideration in the assessment of theories. (This is the claim that factors relevant to discovery are irrelevant to justification.) But it does not follow that the process of science is characterized by distinct evaluative and non-evaluative phases. The absurdity of the notion of the generation of creative ideas as non-evaluative has been demonstrated in considerable detail in the previous chapter. The generation of scientific ideas is very much constrained by rules, in this case the rules which govern the assessment of these ideas. Thus, although it may be the case that considerations related to discovery are irrelevant to justification, nonetheless considerations of justification are very relevant, indeed crucial to discovery.

Hattiangadi has, in fact, effectively argued the impossibility of clearly distinguishing pure contexts of discovery. He demonstrates, using as an example Newton's discovery of gravity, how any idea which might be considered to be in a context of discovery with respect to a new theory is itself part of the context of justification of a previous idea out of which it developed. Thus one ends up with nested contexts of justification, and any pure contexts of discovery become vanishingly small.[30]

Thus we see that in science as well as in art, rules play a central role. We see, that is, that scientific discovery is rational and rule-governed, that there are continuities between theories, and that knowledge and understanding rather than irrational processes are what is important for scientific advance.

## Knowledge and Problem-Solving

Another issue which is related to the ones already discussed in the course of the present chapter concerns the role of knowledge or past experience in creativity. One corollary of the contemporary view is that knowledge in an area is not necessarily beneficial for creativity because too much experience may confine one to the prevalent mode of thinking and operating and prevent one from transcending the framework in question. This is precisely the sentiment expressed by De Bono in the quotation cited at the beginning of the chapter. What is thought to be required for a creative solution to a problem is not more knowledge in an area but rather a perceptual shift or Gestalt switch which brings about an instant restructuring or rearrangement of available information. Too much information can, in fact, be a hindrance to this sort of restructuring.

Illustrations of this perspective are typically drawn from problem-solving, and so it will be instructive to examine some recent empirical investigations of problem-solving which test the assumptions of this view. Weisberg's findings, based both on his own empirical studies and on other key investigations, directly contradict the main tenets of this view. He has found that not only is knowledge not inhibiting to creative problem-solving but that it is what enables creative solutions to be found.[31]

One oft-cited example of the importance of perceptual shifts and the irrelevance of past experience concerns Köhler's experiments with apes. The apes in his experiments were able to discover how to use a hoe to reach an out-of-reach piece of food without any apparent past experience using sticks as tools. This result has been interpreted in terms of a perceptual shift to bring about an insight into the solution. The attempts by Birch to replicate the experimental findings with apes who had been raised from birth, and not captured as Köhler's apes had been, were unsuccessful. Birch's apes, who were known to have had no past experience with sticks, were unable to solve the problem. This leaves open the possibility that Köhler's captured apes had had some form of past experience using sticks previous to capture which helped them to solve the problem.[32]

The other experiments on problem-solving conducted or described by Weisberg also disconfirmed the Gestalt switch account and demonstrated the importance of experience and knowledge. For example, Harlow's experiments with monkeys attempting to solve two-choice discrimination problems demonstrated the role in problem-solving of gradually acquired expertise in solving similar problems.[33] De Groot's studies of chess masters emphasized the importance of detailed knowledge and expertise for creativity in chess.[34] And Weisberg's own experiments indicated that the crucial factor in enabling individuals to change direction in problem-solving and to achieve a novel solution was additional information.[35]

Weisberg acknowledges that there are some cases where the reliance on past experience is misleading because this experience is not really applicable to a current situation.[36] He suggests, however, that these are artificial, trick problems in which apparent similarities hide real differences, and that they are not representative of situations requiring creative solutions. I would go further to suggest that heuristically, the reliance on past experience is still the soundest strategy and that a failure of tried and true techniques or the inapplicability of past experience would give one good reason to question working assumptions and to try something different. Ignoring or downplaying past experience is not what is required but rather exercising critical judgment in the application of what one knows.

## *Summary*

This chapter has confronted the notion, integral to the contemporary view, that creativity is essentially rule-breaking and that rules, skills and knowledge are inhibiting to creative production. It has been argued that, on the contrary, the rules of the discipline and the skills and knowledge connected with them play a central role in creativity.

It has been shown how the rules of performance in the arts, internalized as skills, are crucial for artistic achievement. Such skills are not a matter of blind and automatic performance, but involve considerable thought, flexibility, and the constant possibility of revision. Thus it is the mastery of such skills which allows one the freedom to go on and to make significant contributions.

Similarly in the case of scientific discovery, it is a repertoire of skills and knowledge which forms the basis for eventual groundbreaking achievement in science.

Another way in which rules are important for scientific discovery is in terms of rules of method. Although it is the case that there is no scientific method in the sense of an algorithm for inventing or justifying theories, nonetheless the scientific enterprise is highly governed by rules. It is constrained both by particular methodological rules, many of which remain constant between theories, and by methodological meta-rules which transcend frameworks. These rules not only govern the justification of theories but are relevant to their generation as well.

Knowledge in an area is also crucial for creativity, contrary to the arguments of the contemporary view. Recent experiments dealing with creative problem-solving clearly indicate that it is increased knowledge and expertise in an area which facilitate creative solutions to problems and not some sort of holistic perceptual shift.

It seems clear, then, that rules, skills and knowledge are indispensable to creative achievement. In them is embodied the practice of the discipline at a specific moment and mastery of them is vital to the advancement of the tradition. They need not, then, lock one into an established way of seeing, for it is their mastery which allows one to proceed. This includes the possibility of transcending some of the rules themselves and adding to the knowledge of the tradition.

### NOTES

1. Koestler, *Act of Creation*, p.96.
2. Feyerabend, *Against Method*, p.23.
3. Edward De Bono, *Practical Thinking* (Middlesex: Penguin Books, 1969), p.228.
4. Plato *Ion* 533c-534c.
5. Aristotle *Nicomachean Ethics* IV. 1140a5.
6. Collingwood, *Principles of Art*, p.111.
7. Tomas, "Creativity in Art," p.285; Hausman, *Discourse on Novelty*, pp.10-11.
8. Maitland, "Creativity," p.397.
9. Howard, *Artistry*, p.118.
10. See, for example, Beardsley, "Creation of Art," in L.A. Jacobus, ed., *Aesthetics and the Arts*, p.58; Howard, *Artistry*, p.119.

## Rules, Skills, and Knowledge    107

11. Tomas, "Creativity in Art."
12. Maitland, "Creativity," p.407.
13. Koestler, *Act of Creation*, p.363.
14. William James, *Talks to Teachers on Psychology* (New York: Henry Holt and Company, 1908), p.64.
15. Gilbert Ryle, *The Concept of Mind* (London: Hutchinson of London, 1949), p.42.
16. Ibid., pp.28-29.
17. Israel Scheffler, *Conditions of Knowledge* (Glenview: Scott, Foresman and Company, 1965), p.103.
18. Howard, *Artistry*, p.162.
19. Etienne Gilson, *Painting and Reality* (Princeton: Princeton University Press, 1957), p.31.
20. Michael Polanyi, *Personal Knowledge* (Chicago: University of Chicago Press, 1958), p.143.
21. H. Selye, "What makes basic research basic?" quoted in Kuhn, *Essential Tension*, p.226.
22. Kuhn, *Essential Tension*, p.227.
23. Ibid., p.237.
24. Feyerabend, *Against Method*, p.23.
25. Ibid., p.69.
26. See Siegel, "What Is the Question Concerning the Rationality of Science?"
27. It was Reichenbach who originated this distinction between the context of discovery and the context of justification in order to distinguish considerations related to the generation of claims from those pertaining to their evaluation. Hans Reichenbach, *Experience and Prediction* (Chicago: The University of Chicago Press, 1938).
28. Popper, *Logic of Scientific Discovery*, pp.31-32.
29. See Harvey Siegel, "Justification, Discovery and the Naturalizing of Epistemology," *Philosophy of Science* 47, 2, (1980).
30. Hattiangadi, "Vanishing Context of Discovery."
31. Weisberg, *Creativity*.
32. Ibid., p.46.
33. Ibid., pp.46-47.
34. Ibid., pp.12-13.
35. Ibid., pp.6-12.
36. Weisberg cites water-jar problems, in which three jars of varying sizes must be used to produce a required amount of water. Ibid., pp.42-43, 49-50.

# Chapter V

# THE SOMETHING MORE

THE VIEW of creativity which we have been developing in the course of the preceding chapters connects creativity not with arbitrary novelty, irrational processes, or rule-breaking, but rather with significant achievement viewed as a product of skills, rules and rational processes. It might be objected, however, that this view is inaccurate or at least incomplete in that it fails to capture that mysterious, ineffable aspect which is the very essence of creativity. It might be claimed that there is something more to creativity which the present view cannot explain, or which, perhaps, cannot be explained at all.

What might this additional element be? It is expressed in a variety of ways depending on the context—inspiration, illumination, vision, genius, to name only a few—but it is perhaps best captured by the concept of imagination. It is connected with going beyond the given, with the origination of ideas and the generation of possibilities. This generation of ideas seems particulary mysterious and inexplicable when the ideas work, when they issue in works of art which touch our sensibilities or scientific theories which prove to be fruitful, or when they break bounds and result in innovations. This imaginative element is usually viewed as very distinct and separate from the skills which are involved in producing a creative work, and, indeed, it is this element which makes possible the transcending of skills and rules which characterizes creativity.

In this chapter I shall argue that imagination is indeed crucial for creative achievement, but that it is not an element which is separable from skill and which transcends it. Rather, they are closely interconnected, with imagination manifested in the execution of skill and skill involved in the development of an imaginative vision. Skills are suffused with imagination, as is, in fact, our thinking in general. All intelligent thought and behaviour involves going beyond the given and has an imaginative, generative component which is constrained by skill and judgment. This interplay of skill and imagination is central to the growth and evolution of traditions and thus to how creative achievement is possible.

## *Art and the Something More*

The claim is sometimes made that skills and imagination are separate elements in artistic activity and that what is required for artistic creativity is a combination of skill, which has nothing to do with imagination, and imagination, which has nothing to do with skill. It would thus be possible for an artist to be skilful but not at all imaginative, or imaginative but not at all skilful.

In order to assess the appropriateness of this radical separation between imagination and skill, it is necessary, first, to gain a clearer understanding of what is meant by the imaginative element in art. It is a feature often referred to in a variety of ways in talk about art, Pope's 'grace beyond the reach of art', for example.[1] A wonderful expression of this separation of imagination and skill is provided by the dramatic monologue "Andrea del Sarto" by Robert Browning. In this monologue Andrea del Sarto, who is recognized by his contemporaries for his amazing technical skill, expresses the belief that his work is yet lacking something, be it called inspiration or soul or whatever. Of other artists who strive for perfection but whose work is less technically proficient than his own, Andrea says:

> Well, less is more, Lucrezia: I am judged.
> There burns a truer light of God in them,
> In their vexed, beating, stuffed and stopped-up brain,
> Heart, or whate'er else, than goes on to prompt
> This low-pulsed forthright craftsman's hand of mine.

And of a work by Raphael he states:

> Well, I can fancy how he did it all,
> Pouring his soul, with kings and popes to see,
> Reaching, that heaven might so replenish him,
> Above and through his art—for it gives way:
> That arm is wrongly put—and there again—
> A fault to pardon in the drawing's lines,
> Its body, so to speak: its soul is right,
> He means right—that, a child could understand.
> Still, what an arm! and I could alter it:
> But all the play, the insight and the stretch—
> Out of me, out of me! And wherefore out? (78-117)

The idea which is expressed through the character of del Sarto is that there is an element, variously referred to as soul, stretch, insight, and a truer light of God, which is independent of technical proficiency and indeed technical mastery, and which is responsible for the greatness of works of art. The claim is that, although an artist may have extreme skill in accurately portraying, say, the human body, nonetheless the painting which results from this skill may be lacking. The question then arises as to what this element is which is lacking.

If art is viewed as always involving interpretation of some kind, as involving seeing from a certain perspective or 'seeing as', then one possibility is that the vision which is expressed through a particular interpretation constitutes this additional imaginative element. This is perhaps most evident in realistic forms of visual art and in literature. In works in these genres, images of human experience are created through the choice of subject and how precisely it is portrayed. Sometimes these images touch us, move us, reveal insights to which we can relate. They may create images of an emotional, spiritual, or erotic nature which strike a respondent chord or evoke symbols with universal appeal. If works of art achieve this, then this might be what prompts us to attribute to them this additional quality. The insight or vision conveyed in these works might be brand new and constitute a novel way of viewing a phenomenon or experience. Thus a work of art may provide a new perspective and allow us to see something differently than previously. Or it may touch us because it provides an apt expression for something which we ourselves have already felt or perceived, but which has remained unarticulated.

Can this notion of vision or insight as the something more be applied to art in which there is no subject or content in quite the way that there is in representational painting or literature—abstract painting or music, for example? One might question whether a work by Bach or a painting by Mondrian could really be said to express an insight into human nature or vision of human experience. In such artistic genres, what is primary is the manner in which formal elements are combined. Nonetheless, such works might still be said to express a vision in some sense, although not in the literal sense described previously. In striving after a principle such as purity or simplicity, in manipulating sensuous elements such as colour, tone, or rhythm, these works may touch our sensibilities in such a way that we attribute to them imagination.

This imaginative element is also evident in the performing arts. In music, it might be used to characterize the difference between playing an instrument mechanically and exhibiting insight in the execution of a piece of music. The latter would be manifested in the manner in which the piece is interpreted and in the expression which is thereby evoked. There are always numerous judgments to be made regarding such features as rhythm, tempo, and phrasing, and particular choices might create effects which are deemed especially effective. A musician might, for example, impose a particular rhythm on a piece which gives it a sense of unity previously unexplored; she might use a fraction of a moment's hesitation to produce a heightened sense of anticipation; or she might impose a tempo which is different from that normally used and which reveals new possibilities for the work. These types of interpretations, when they are deemed particularly effective, might constitute what is meant by the something more in musical performance.

These factors of interpretation and expression also exist in the theatrical arts, and are connected here as well with what is meant by imagination. In acting, for example, a distinction is often drawn between acting purely technically and acting in an imaginative manner. The former refers to acting which is superficial and relies on a repertoire of hackneyed gestures and responses, acting which lacks depth, genuine feeling, and true insight into the character portrayed. Superior acting, on the other hand, involves the creation of a unique and believable character and involves depth of feeling and real understanding. It is often pointed out that an actor may be technically proficient in terms of skills of presentation and performance, but yet lack these other elements.

The notion of interpretation is centrally important in the area of directing as well. The director's job is essentially that of working out an interpretation of a script which will be realized in the concrete terms of the production and communicated to the audience. If this is done in a manner which is just like other productions of the play, if no new elements are introduced save those explicitly stated in the script, if the dramatic values inherent in the play are not enhanced by the production, then the directing would be seen to be dull and unimaginative. If, on the other hand, the production fills out the script in novel ways so as to enhance the dramatic values, if new insights into the play are created through the interpretation, then we might want to say that the directing is inspired or imaginative.

Sometimes this something more refers to the imagination or vision which allows an artist to transcend an existing artistic framework and to create radically new forms or a new style, technique, or school of art. It is often believed that one can exercise masterful skill in working within a framework and following existing rules well, but that something more than skill is required in order to create new rules and new standards for judgment. This special imagination or vision is also cited in instances of creative problem-solving in any domain. There are, after all, numerous ways to solve most problems, but some ways seem to be more interesting, more innovative, more imaginative than others. It is often thought that although two individuals are equally knowledgeable and proficient in a specific area, one might be more imaginative and thus more likely to generate solutions to problems which would be considered creative.

To this point, we have examined a number of kinds of cases in which we would want to attribute imagination, and for which it is often claimed that something special and mysterious is at work, something which transcends skills. Let us examine such cases more closely, however, and attempt to determine to what extent there really is something more than skills involved.

First, it seems to be the case that this view of imagination as separate from and transcending skills presupposes a very limited sense of the notion of skill. It assumes that skill is confined to a certain sort of technical proficiency which is applied mechanically and in a repetitive manner, and that judgments go beyond skills. As has been demonstrated previously, however, this is simply not the case. There are many sorts of skills, some relatively simple, but others highly complex. The latter higher order skills are not a matter simply of proficiency in certain techniques, but rather of very sophisticated mastery based on a repertoire of lower order skills. This involves the integration of lower order skills, and considerable judgment.

The notion of skills thus elaborated can be of considerable help in attempting to understand the imaginative element evident in artistic creation. To what extent does this imaginative dimension of creative work truly involve something more than skill taken in this broader sense? Let us look, first, at the Andrea del Sarto case. The assumption here is that, although del Sarto is more skilful than Raphael, yet Raphael is the superior artist in terms of the imaginative vision which he embodies in his works. One might question, however, whether del Sarto really is more skilful. Even if he were more proficient in the limited sense of having more technical proficiency in accurately portraying the human body, nonetheless surely Raphael's ability to portray his figures with certain expressions which have a special effect on the viewer is part of a higher order skill. Judgments relating to composition, colour, line, light and shade, brush strokes and so on come into play in the creation of effects and in the manner in which the subject is portrayed.

Moreover, even the notion of accurate portrayal is problematic. Del Sarto indicates that Raphael's lack of technical expertise is shown by an arm 'wrongly put', a fault which he himself could easily correct, but that despite such faults in the 'body' of the painting, its 'soul' is right. Yet one might certainly question whether, if del Sarto had actually corrected the faulty arm, the 'soul' of the painting would have remained intact. Surely the expressive possibility of a painting is not something added on to an accurate portrayal, but is an integral part of the manner in which a subject is portrayed. Painting always involves some degree of 'seeing as' — of interpretation and of transformation, and the conveying of a certain perspective will involve emphasizing some aspects over others. The Impressionists, for example, may have abandoned the accuracy of line and shape of their predecessors, but what they were able to achieve thereby was an unrivalled accuracy in the portrayal of natural light. As another example, in the sculptures of Michelangelo, certain features tend to be exaggerated beyond realistic proportions, but this is certainly not a technical fault in the work. On the contrary, it is precisely by means of these exaggerations that the remarkable emotional intensity of the works is achieved. Wight makes this point with reference to the Pieta:

> The Madonna appears as a young girl and we do not immediately notice that she is on a larger than life scale, cradling the figure of Christ as though he were still a child. It is always in Michelangelo's exaggeration that the emotion lies.[2]

This discussion seems to point to the conclusion that there is a problem with the view that the artist begins with a vision which is subsequently executed, the vision being a product of imagination and the execution a product of skill. This radical separation of imagination and skill is, in fact, problematic. It is not the case that the artist possesses a full-blown imaginative vision totally independent of the skills constitutive of the art. Rather, higher-order skills necessarily involve imagination and these skills contribute to and are an integral part of the development of the imaginative vision. This is a point which Gombrich ably demonstrates with reference to the visual arts. He shows how the skills, techniques, and even materials which an artist employs will contribute to how a subject is seen and portrayed.[3] The manner in which a subject is seen and portrayed is precisely what we mean by the artistic vision, and so skills are necessarily involved in the development of this vision. The skills of the art, then, are not something totally separate from the imagination embodied in a vision which is in place before the skills come into play. Rather, there is imagination manifested in the execution of skill, and also skill involved in the development of the imaginative vision.

This point can be demonstrated as well with reference to literature. We might want to connect the imagination reflected in a specific poem with the insight into humanity which is expressed — with the relationships, the emotion, the vision. Yet this vision is expressed in the choice of words and their combination and juxtaposition, in the metaphors and similes, in the images created. All of these relate to the skill of the poet as well as to her imagination. It would be somewhat misleading, then, to say that the imaginative vision is expressed by means of the poet's skilled use of language. Rather, the former is developed through the latter. The vision is a poetic vision, and the imagination of the poet is a poetic imagination.

This role of skill in the imagination displayed in a work is perhaps even more striking in the case of non-representational works. In the case of music, for example, it seems clear that the imaginative component does not consist in a vision conceived apart from the music itself, but rather resides in the manner in which the various formal elements are combined and the music made. The vision, if we want to think in these terms, is a musical vision and is thus closely connected with the skills of the composer.

In the case of the performing arts, this wider applicability of the notion of skill can be seen, as well. We stated, above, that the imaginative something more is exhibited in music in the manner in which a piece is interpreted and the expression thereby created. Such expression is essentially a product of the choices made with regard to features such as rhythm, tempo, phrasing, and so on, and these choices are a product of the judgment of the musician. A musician who is seen to play mechanically might be one who plays works precisely as she has been taught them or has heard them played. One who is seen to play imaginatively would be one whose interpretations are unique and effective. The latter factor is particularly important as not any innovation will be judged as imaginative. The musician who exhibits something more in his playing, then, will be the one who has such highly developed musical judgment and skill that the choices he makes in interpretation will reveal new possibilities in a work and render it highly effective. The one who plays mechanically is not exercising a similar degree of musical judgment or skill.

The situation is parallel in the case of acting. The contrasting of acting purely technically and acting with imagination is based on a narrow sense of the term technique. If the notion of technique is limited to movement on stage, control of the voice and body, projection, and similar abilities, then the ability to act imaginatively and effectively must be viewed as something more. Yet surely the ability to understand a character and to create a believable presence on stage is a part of the actor's skill as well. Such a characterization comes not purely from a pre-existing abstract vision, but rather from the actor working with the script, director, and other actors and developing the characterization through technical abilities and acting skills. Once this is recognized, we can see here again that the notions of imagination and skill are not easily separated.

The same holds true in the case of directing. We view the imaginative element in directing as reflected in the interpretation which is embodied in the production, and this interpretation is very much a product of the director's skill. The director must bring out the dramatic values inherent in the script, and doing so is largely a matter of solving the problems which the script presents. What emerges in the actual production as the director's imaginative vision is not, then, an arbitrary flight of fantasy, but is a carefully worked through whole based on work with the script and the actors, knowledge of dramatic principles, and dramatic problem-solving abilities.

Let us now look at the claim that something more than skills is required in the case of an artist who does not simply work well within an existing tradition but who develops a new style, technique or form and thus new standards for judgment. Our discussions in the two previous chapters have, I believe, shown that the ability to work at the highest level within a framework and the ability to transcend a framework are not radically different but are part of a continuum. We have demonstrated that judgment is not limited to working within a confined frame of reference and that we need not invoke some highly mysterious and extraordinary power apart from extremely highly developed skill in the broad sense in which we are using it to explain the transcending of frameworks. This point is eloquently expressed by Sparshott in his description of the truly creative artist as:

> the one whose style determines a way of developing and changing his ways of proceeding themselves, who sees in the next occasion for his art not an opportunity to do what he knows how to do but an opportunity to do what he knows to be the next thing.[4]

What the preceding discussion has shown is that once the nature of skills in highly sophisticated performances is recognized, they can go a considerable distance in helping to explain the elusive 'something more'. It must be realized that skills and imagination cannot be neatly separated but are parts of the same process and develop together in the creation of a product.

Yet it might be objected at this point that this account is still inadequate in that some highly skilled artists may have very little to say while others will begin with a richness of imagery and perceptions, insights into humanity and depths of emotion which fuel their imagination and give a special life to their work. Freud's account of the role of the unconscious as a source of creativity provides an example of this type of view. Freud claims that unfulfilled wishes and desires residing in the unconscious are at the source of fantasy and that artistic endeavours such as creative writing are essentially an extension of such fantasy. He says of the process of creative writing:

> A strong experience in the present awakens in the creative writer a memory of an earlier experience (usually belonging to his childhood) from which there now proceeds a wish which finds its fulfilment in the creative work.[5]

Freud relates the fact that the spectator is moved or affected by works of art to the fact that the works connect with the spectator's own unfulfilled wishes and desires. The latter are, however, adorned and disguised sufficiently that the spectator can overcome natural feelings of repulsion toward them and can enjoy the works without shame. For Freud, the writer's *ars poetica* is really the technique whereby these shameful feelings are disguised, making them acceptable, and giving the reader an aesthetic fore-pleasure which allows for involvement in the work in order to experience the real pleasure which arises from 'deeper psychological sources'. It is his opinion that:

> all the aesthetic pleasure which a creative writer affords us has the character of a fore-pleasure of this kind, and our actual enjoyment of an imaginative work proceeds from a liberation of tensions in our minds.[6]

It does seem to be the case that past experiences, especially those of childhood, unfulfilled wishes, desires, fears, and emotions generally, have provided the source for many works of art. Tennessee Williams's desperately unhappy childhood and his homosexuality, for example, were doubtless the seminal force for many of his plays. And Leonardo's manner of portraying women has been linked, by Freud, to his obsession with the smile of his mother and all the repressed feelings that it evoked for him. The painter Ben Shahn provides a striking description of the genesis of one of his paintings, "Allegory", which depicts a fiery lion-like beast perched over the bodies of several children. He outlines the multiplicity of factors which contributed to the development of the work, including a contemporary fire, the memories of several fires in his childhood and the terror which accompanied them, and the images of wolves and their mythical and emotional associations for him. The following, for example, is his account of the creating of a symbol for a deeply experienced emotion:

> Of one of these, a lion-like head, but still not a lion, I made many drawings, each drawing approaching more nearly some inner figure of primitive terror which I was seeking to capture.[7]

This noting of the role of subconscious, repressed emotions as sources of artistic imagination was an important contribution of Freud's. Nonetheless, his theory has severe limitations as an account of creativity. First, it must be recognized that the extent to which these unconscious factors play a role varies from art to art and even from work to work. They are clearly evident in many works of literature and some representational paintings. But it would be much more difficult to make a case for their influence in some landscapes, abstract paintings, or musical works. It does not seem plausible to see a painting of Mondrian's or a work of Bach's as primarily expressions of childhood traumas or infantile desires. Of course psychologically prominent events have sometimes provided inspiration for great musical works, Mahler's *Kindertotenlieder*, for example, and the works of many nineteenth century Romantic composers, Schumann for example, are marked by considerable emotional effusion. It would be a mistake, however, to view music primarily as expression of emotion, as Hanslick has pointed out. In addressing the question of whether music is capable of representing any definite emotion, he replies:

> To this question only a negative answer can be given, the definiteness of an emotion being inseparably connected with concrete notions and conceptions, and to reduce these to a material form is altogether beyond the power of music.[8]

The construction of a musical work has more to do with the manipulation of formal elements. As Hanslick further states:

> The ideas which a composer expresses are mainly and primarily of a purely musical nature.[9]

This last point underlines the major problem with psychoanalytic theories such as Freud's in giving an account of creativity. They may contribute to the understanding of the sources of imagination for some works of art, but they cannot explain the actual creation of a work of art. The skill or *ars poetica* which Freud relegates to the category of adornment and disguise is, in fact, central to this creation. Even Ben Shahn, while recognizing the importance of psychological factors, makes this point:

> The subconscious may greatly shape one's art; undoubtedly it does so. But the subconscious cannot create art. The very act of making a painting is an intending one.[10]

We doubtless all have fantasies and unfulfilled wishes, but we are not all artists. Freud may also be correct that one of the reasons that some works of art affect the spectator so deeply is connected with the fact that they touch on hidden fears, desires, and emotions. They are able to touch the spectator in a particular way, however, not simply because they relate to desires and so on, but because they are art—because they take a particular form, a form which has aesthetic impact. Reading *Crime and Punishment* is very different from listening to someone recounting a daydream.

## *Science and the Something More*

Let us now turn to the realm of science to see how the something more of creativity is thought to be manifested in this domain. Imagination is considered to be centrally involved in the invention of hypotheses and theories. Skill and judgment are considered crucial to the evaluation of theories once they have been invented, but the actual generation of the theories in the first place is relegated, by many philosophers of science, to the ranks of the inexplicable, the mysterious, the intuitive. Thus Popper states:

> The initial stage, the act of conceiving or inventing a theory, seems to me neither to call for logical analysis nor to be susceptible of it.[11]

And later:

> there is no such thing as a logical method of having new ideas, or a logical reconstruction of this process. My view may be expressed by saying that every discovery contains 'an irrational element', or a 'creative intuition', in Bergson's sense.[12]

Another place claimed for imagination in science is in terms of discoveries or advances which break boundaries, which overthrow existing presuppositions, which create new frameworks and new paradigms according to which science is practised. Discoveries such as the Copernican theory of planetary motion or Einstein's theory of relativity would be examples. In these cases, the scientist is not simply solving problems for which the method of solution is well delineated by the existing scientific paradigm but is, rather, combining elements in a novel way, resulting in a new way of viewing the problem, and thereby changing the paradigm. It is often argued that in order to accomplish this, such scientists must be exhibiting something more than skill—that they must have a special sort of imagination or vision.

The problem with this notion of imagination as transcending skill in science is analogous to the problem we encountered previously with respect to art. In both cases a strict separation is made between skill and imagination, and this dichotomy is as misleading for scientific discovery as it is for artistic creation. The generation of scientific hypotheses and theories is not totally free, unconstrained and irrational but is highly constrained by rules and hence by the judgment and skill of the practitioner who adheres to these rules. Hypotheses and theories arise in the context of scientific problems and have to meet the requirements of the problem situation. And, as Hattiangadi has pointed out, problems do not arise in isolation but rather in the context of solutions to previous problems. Thus there is a whole constellation of constraints affecting the invention of theories.[13]

The preceding applies as much to the invention of theories which are revolutionary and which establish new paradigms as it does to the invention of theories which remain largely within the existing paradigm. The discussions in the previous chapters have demonstrated that there is continuity between paradigms, that there are rules which govern scientific discovery even in cases of revolutionary discovery, and that the ability to work at the most highly skilled level within a framework and the ability to transcend frameworks are not radically different but are part of a continuum. Skill, as elaborated in the previous chapter, involves imagination, flexibility, judgment and the continual possibility for revision, and thus there is no need to posit some mysterious, irrational power apart from extremely highly developed skill and judgment in order to explain even the invention of those theories which transcend frameworks.

## *Generation and Criticism*

The emphasis on the importance of skill in the preceding analysis of creativity is not meant to imply that there is no place for imagination. The generation of ideas, exploration and free play are all central to creative activity. The main point of the account, however, is that the free play of ideas is never really totally free, that there are constraints on what ideas are generated, that evaluation and criticism are very much aspects of imaginative invention. This is a point which has been argued for and emphasized throughout this work.

The additional point that must be stressed at the present juncture is that the reverse is also true. Evaluation and criticism involve imagination. Thus the radical distinction which is drawn by the contemporary view between the generation of ideas and their evaluation and execution is faulty on two counts. First, it mistakenly assumes that the generation of ideas is non-judgmental. But it also assumes that the judgment involved in evaluating and executing ideas is mechanical and algorithmic. This view is well characterized by Scheffler as follows:

> It will be granted that *discipline* is indeed only one aspect of science and art, to be supplemented by *freedom* in creation. Once freedom has been exercised, however, then discipline alone comes into play. So arises a familiar division between pure and applied science, and an analogous separation of inspiration and execution in art. In science, free play is conceded a place in the generation of theory, but not in its application. Once a theory is available, applying it becomes a matter of disciplined intelligence or skill merely, and teleological rationality rules....Similarly—in the spirit of Collingwood's separation of art from craft—the artist is conceded freedom in conceiving his basic idea, but once the idea is available, the rest is merely a matter of disciplined execution, a display of technical prowess at best.[14]

The idea that the execution of ideas is a strictly mechanical and automatic procedure is also seriously flawed, however. It would imply that the creator has complete and perfect knowledge of how the product will turn out before even beginning the process of execution, but we have seen the problems with this view in the preceding chapter. It was demonstrated that, in the case of the artist, the degree of foreknowledge varies considerably. Sometimes an artist will begin a work with only a vague and general idea, and the artistic idea is developed in the very process of creating the work. Thus the process of creation is very much more than simply the mechanical execution of a pre-existing idea. Imagination is very much involved in the process of execution, and, indeed, the very division of the process of artistic creation into separate phases of generation and execution is highly misleading.

Even when a creator does begin a work with a detailed advanced plan, however, the execution is not simply a mechanical exercise because things do not always go as planned. There is always the

## The Something More  123

possibility of the breakdown of our theories and surprise can never be ruled out, as Scheffler points out:

> human creation is always contingent, always experimental, always capable of yielding surprises—not only for others, but for the human creator himself. The product humanly made is never a pure function of creative purpose and foreseeable consequences of the maker's actions.[15]

The process of execution involves testing ideas, evaluating them, dealing with and learning from surprises and unforeseen consequences and developments, and making changes in the original plan or idea based on what is learnt. Thus the process of creating, rather than being characterized by phases of imaginative generation and subsequent mechanical execution is best seen as much more of an interaction between the creator's original idea or intention and the work itself as it develops and evolves. Maitland's description of a work of art as growing out of a dialogue between the artist and his forehavings on the one hand and the emerging work of art on the other captures well this process.[16] And this interactive process of creating is applicable to scientific work as well. Scientists do not always begin their research with a clearly formulated problem which they then proceed to solve according to a mechanical method. Rather, problems frequently become clarified and reformulated in the process of being worked out. This point is made by Scheffler with respect to artistic creation, but he clearly states that it applies as well for scientific applications, for policy making, and for everyday activities:

> The artist is not a composite of dreamer and robot, the dreamer intuiting the idea and the robot executing it automatically in the chosen medium. The painter or composer does not first thrill to a new conception and then thoughtlessly stamp it on his raw material; rather, he tries it out on the material, which reshapes him as he reshapes it. His thinking is not limited to the first phase of his making; it permeates every stage, the results of his every move requiring fresh evaluation and a reconsideration of basic directions.[17]

Imagination in the form of the generation of new ideas and the reshaping of existing ones takes place throughout the entire process of creating. Thinking permeates every stage of the process of making, and this thinking has an imaginative, generative aspect.

The belief that the generation of creative ideas is highly mysterious and inexplicable may be connected with the failure to recognize this generative aspect to thinking in general. The generation of ideas which are effective and fruitful is a puzzling phenomenon only if it is viewed as out of the ordinary, as contrary to the way we normally think, and thus as in need of special explanation. Yet all our intelligent thought has a generative aspect. This is the point of Bruner's remark, cited earlier, that going beyond the information given is an important aspect of all our thinking and is not limited to instances of creation.

Thus even thinking which is primarily directed to the criticism and evaluation of ideas is not devoid of imagination. It is not merely analytic, selective, and confined within frameworks, but has imaginative, inventive, constructive aspects. An example can be drawn from the area of critical thinking and informal reasoning. Critical thinking involves assessing information, arguments or actions on the basis of reasons, but such assessments are seldom clear-cut or mechanical. They require an imaginative contribution on the part of the assessor. Identifying assumptions, inventing hypotheses, generating counter-examples and constructing counter-arguments are all aspects of informal reasoning which require imagination. As Ennis has pointed out, such reasoning activities as observing, inferring, conceiving alternatives, and offering a well organized line of reasoning are all activities in which

> the thinker contributes more than evaluation to the result.[18]

And Scriven sums up this point nicely when he states:

> the very process of criticism necessarily involves the creative activity of generating new theories or hypotheses to explain phenomena that have seemed to other people to admit of only one explanation.[19]

Moreover, critical thinking involves more than assessing isolated arguments, actions or pieces of information according to clearly-defined criteria and using specifiable techniques, as Paul has pointed out.[20] In actual instances of critical reasoning, it is rarely the case that we pass definitive judgment on isolated arguments. Rather, we judge between conflicting points of view, and adjudicate among competing arguments. And certainly the criteria of informal logic provide one basis for so doing. Yet such criteria are seldom decisive in and of themselves, and what the reasoner must do is to construct a new view which resolves the problems posed by the conflicting views and synthesize the soundest aspects of each into a new and coherent whole. This dialectical aspect of critical thinking clearly requires imagination and invention.

This generative aspect to critical thought is also evident in thinking within traditional subject areas. Making assessments and solving problems within traditional disciplines are seldom automatic procedures. Rather, the reasoner must go beyond the confines of the given information, supplying imaginative constructs. Perkins makes this point with respect to mathematics:

> The evident challenge posed by many mathematical problems plainly calls upon the problem solver's powers of invention. To be sure, if a mathematical problem allows a solution by sheer guesswork or systematic computation, with no need to discover a path from given to answer, then imagination need play no role. But virtually all serious mathematical problems do not surrender so easily, else they would not count as serious.[21]

The fundamental idea which provides the grounding for the common view of creativity is that our thinking normally takes place within fixed frameworks and is analytic and evaluative but non-generative and that a special kind of thinking is required to transcend frameworks, thinking which is generative but non-judgmental. This view creates a picture of traditional disciplines as static, discontinuous bodies of information and procedures which are bound by rules which apply within frameworks but not between them. Creativity, then, cannot be explained by any processes inherent in disciplines but instead requires the postulation of extraordinary, irrational processes which are external to disciplines.

This picture misunderstands at a very fundamental level the nature and structure of disciplines, however. They are not static, fixed bodies of information and procedures. Rather, they are traditions of knowledge and inquiry which are open-ended and dynamic. They consist not merely in information but also in live questions and modes of investigating these questions. And even the bodies of facts are not fixed but are in flux. There are open questions, ongoing debates, and areas of controversy within every discipline, and these furnish the arena for evolution and change.

Traditions evolve continually, and this change grows out of the attempt to deal with the problems inherent in the tradition as well as in response to various influences in society and culture. Truly creative innovation, change which is effective, useful, and significant is not a product of arbitrary novelty, of uninformed intuition, but emerges, rather, out of a profound understanding of the nature of the tradition and of its principles. This point is expressed eloquently by Scheffler:

> We need not pretend that these principles of ours are immutable or innate. It is enough that they are what we ourselves acknowledge, that they are the best we know, and that we are prepared to improve them should the need and occasion arise. Such improvement is possible, however, only if we succeed in passing on, too, the multiple live traditions in which they are embodied, and in which a sense of their history, spirit, and direction may be discerned.[22]

Emphasizing that the mechanisms for criticism and thereby for change are built right into traditions themselves in no way implies that creativity is limited to traditional disciplines. Outstanding achievements are possible at the interface between two disciplines, in a hybrid field which results from a cross-fertilization between disciplines, or in areas of human activity which do not fall neatly into any one of the traditional disciplines. Nonetheless, knowledge and modes of inquiry which arise from our traditional disciplines generally provide the basis for the creative outcomes in these areas. And the examples of outstanding achievement which we consider prototypical of creativity are generally drawn from the arts, sciences and humanities—from the inherited traditions of human inquiry and achievement.

## *Emotion and Attitude*

It might be objected that the account of creativity which is being developed here with its emphasis on traditions of inquiry and rational processes of thought fails to allow for the affective component of creative activity. Emotion, it might be argued, is central to creativity but it is excluded from an account which stresses the rationality of creative endeavour. This is emphatically not the case, however.

The idea that an account which emphasizes rationality leaves no room for emotion is based on the belief that reason and emotion are necessarily in opposition one to another. This is clearly erroneous. Reason and emotion are, in fact, very closely intertwined. Reasoned assessments are at the basis for many emotions and cognition is necessarily suffused with emotion.

Scheffler has pointed out a number of ways in which emotions play a role in cognition,[23] and several of these cognitive emotions are important for creativity. There are emotions which are connected with the life of reason, rational passions (as they are called by Peters[24]) such as love of truth, repugnance of distortion and evasion, and respect for the arguments of others, and these emotions are crucial for the pursuit of inquiry.

In addition, emotions are often centrally involved in our critical appraisals of situations and in our selection and application of ideas as well as their generation. This does not imply that we are or ought to be governed in our rational choices by irrational emotions, but rather that certain emotions have come to be connected with rational assessments and can thus provide cues for future assessments.[25] This seems to be very much how the phenomenon of intuition operates. As we have seen previously, high-order skill and judgment often become assimilated and operate below the level of conscious awareness. Thus, when confronted with a problem situation, one may at first be aware only of an emotional impetus to investigate in a certain direction without any explicit awareness of the judgments which underlie this feeling. Yet the emotion is doubtless connected with previous successful assessments and these levels of skill and judgment which have been assimilated and are not conscious or explicit.

Finally, Scheffler outlines two emotions which he views as specifically cognitive, the joy of verification and the feeling of surprise. The joy of verification is that feeling of elation which occurs when one's predictions are proven correct, and this emotion is likely an important motivational factor for the conduct of scientific inquiry. The feeling of surprise is, for Scheffler, a central emotional component of creative activity. Surprise results when an occurrence conflicts with our prior expectations. Such conflict is an intrinsic and necessary part of the process of creation because there are always breakdowns in our theories and we can never predict exactly how our creations will turn out. What is crucial then, according to Scheffler, is how one reacts to surprise. The attitude most conducive to creativity is an openness to surprise, a receptivity to the uncertainty which is thereby entailed, and a commitment to learning from the new developments. Surprise may be transformed into wonder and curiosity, and these provide the prime impetus to creative achievement. This is a point which Scheffler stresses:

> Curiosity replaces the impact of surprise with the demand for explanation; it turns confusion into question....Critical inquiry in pursuit of explanation is a constructive outcome of surprise, transforming initial disorientation into motivated search.[26]

Our traditions of knowledge are, then, embodiments of this critical process of inquiry in which the solutions to problems give rise to new problems which are the source for continual motivated search and thus for creative evolution.

## *Fostering Creativity*

Much of the impetus for contemporary research into creativity arises from the belief that creativity is something which ought to be developed and which, indeed, can be developed. Thus it seems appropriate to summarize our findings by indicating what the implications are of the present account for the fostering of creativity.

The contemporary view of creativity which has been the object of our scrutiny makes certain claims which form the basis for a set of educational practices aimed at fostering creativity. According to this view, there is a distinctive creative process of thought which is different from ordinary, logical thinking and which is characterized by the generation of novelty, by leaps of imagination, by rule-breaking, and by irrational processes. Such processes are necessary in order to transcend the conceptual strictures of frameworks and to generate radical novelty. Being creative, then, involves possessing the cognitive and personality traits such as fluency, flexibility and non-conformity which make one good at the creative process, and is not necessarily connected with the production of products.

This view of creativity has had very clear manifestations in educational practice. One outcome has been a proliferation of techniques and courses which purport to foster creativity through an emphasis on novelty, the suspension of judgment, the spontaneous generation of ideas, and irrational processes. It has also resulted in attempts to teach creativity as an isolated psychological process considered independently of specific disciplinary contexts. Another result has been a stress on the development of certain personality characteristics and a simultaneous move away from the encouragement of significant achievement. And it has resulted in the downplaying of skills and knowledge within disciplinary areas.

The numerous problems with this contemporary view have been demonstrated in the course of the present work. One problem is that this view is based on a mistaken assimilation of creativity to the generation of radical novelty seen as discontinuous with the past and thus not amenable to evaluation. It has been shown, however, that there are always continuities between creative works and the traditions out of which they emerge, and, moreover, that it is really the significance of creative works as judged against the background of these traditions that is important.

It has also been argued that there is not a distinctive creative process which is different from ordinary, rational processes of thought, but that the process of creating just is the process of excellent thinking and performing in an area. If this is the case, then the notion of creativity being connected with personality traits rather than with actual creating is incoherent. We must look for creativity not in an isolatable psychological process but rather in palpable achievements within dynamic traditions.

This type of creative achievement presupposes skill—not simply low level skill applied mechanically, but rather higher order skill involving considerable judgment. The more skilful one is in terms of making high order judgments in the discipline, the greater will be the possibility that one will reach a point where one sees the necessity for and has the ability to make changes in the rules of the discipline itself.

The imagination which is an important component in creativity cannot be viewed apart from such skill. Rather, one's skills in an area shape and constrain one's imagination and these skills themselves have an imaginative component. It is this interplay between skill and imagination which accounts for the evolution and development of traditions and thus to how creative achievement comes about.

If the contemporary view of creativity is thus seriously flawed, then the educational prescriptions based on it are fundamentally misdirected. Creative achievement is not likely to result from attempting to foster certain personality traits such as fluency or flexibility nor from encouraging the resistance to judgment, rule-breaking, flights of fancy and irrationality. Rather, it is more likely to emerge through the encouragement of knowledge, skills, and critical thought within alive and dynamic traditions. This is not to imply that techniques such as brainstorming or the random stimulation of ideas have no place at all. They might be useful in particular circumstances, where excess rigidity is a problem or a block is encountered. But seeing them as the way to teach people to be creative is a mistake.

Moreover, there is no one trait which is definitive of creativity. Although flexibility might be helpful in some circumstances, it might be a hindrance in others in terms of giving up an idea prematurely and not working out the implications or solving accompanying problems. Similarly, fluency is not necessarily what is required for creative achievement since it is ultimately the quality and not the quantity of ideas which matters. And rule-following is as important for creativity as is rule-breaking. What is crucial, however, is knowing when to follow and when to break rules.

The last point indicates the vital importance of knowledge and skill for creativity. Such skill and knowledge are not inhibiting, but rather open the way for creative achievement. High order skills are not merely mechanized habits but involve critical judgment applied in a variety of changing circumstances. Thus the teaching of skills as flexible abilities related to ends which may vary might obviate the possibility of rigidity and mechanization.

In addition, the knowledge which is crucial to creative achievement is much more than merely an acquaintance with a body of facts. It involves, as well, an in-depth understanding of the principles and procedures of the discipline in question, of the method whereby inquiry proceeds, of the standards according to which reasons are assessed, and of the over-all goals and deep questions which are at issue. Central to this is an understanding of traditions not as static and fixed collections of information, but rather as modes of inquiry containing open questions, areas of controversy and ongoing debates. Mechanisms for criticism and thereby for change are an intrinsic part of any discipline. Thus criticism must be understood as part of the subject matter itself, as part of what it means to learn a discipline, as the method whereby inquiry proceeds. And it must be understood that the possibility for evolution and innovation is afforded by the critical and dynamic nature of disciplines and does not require an abandonment of disciplinary skills nor a reliance on irrational processes.

The attitude which is most conducive to this orientation to knowledge and traditions and ultimately to creative achievement is summed up by McKellar as follows:

> serious receptivity towards previous thought products and unwillingness to accept them as final.[27]

Taking previous thought products seriously implies recognizing the importance of knowledge and skills, of judgment, and of in-depth understanding in creative production. Unwillingness to accept such products as final entails an understanding of the dynamic, lively, evolutionary nature of traditions and the critical nature of inquiry. This avoids both the extremes of blind obedience to authority and tradition, which can only result in stagnation, and of wholesale rejection of tradition, which can lead nowhere.

The basic conclusion of the present investigation is that the contemporary view is fundamentally mistaken in seeing creativity in terms of arbitrary novelty, rule-breaking, unfettered imagination, and irrational processes. Rather, creativity has to do with significant achievement and such achievement takes place against the background of dynamic and evolving traditions of knowledge and inquiry. It involves rule-following as well as rule-breaking and an understanding of when to do each. It involves skills deployed with imagination and imagination directed by skill. And it employs rational processes of thought which involve judgment, criticism and hence the possibility for evolution. In short, creativity has to do with actual creating and with quality production, and it is vital that we bear this in mind. It is crucial, as well, that we continue to promote the development of the traditions of knowledge and culture which are the arenas of human creative achievement.

### NOTES

1. A. Pope, "An Essay on Criticism," in W.J. Bates, ed., *Criticism: The Major Texts* (New York: Harcourt Brace Jovanovich, 1970), p.174.
2. Wight, *Potent Image*, p.119.
3. Gombrich, *Art and Illusion*. See, especially, Chapter II.

4. F. Sparshott, "Every Horse Has a Mouth: A Personal Poetics," in D. Dutton and M. Krausz, eds., *The Concept of Creativity in Science and Art* (The Hague: Martinus Nijhoff, 1981), pp.51-52.

5. Sigmund Freud, "Creative Writers and Day-Dreaming," in J.Stachey, ed., *Standard Edition of the Complete Psychological Works of Sigmund Freud*, vol. 9 (Hogarth Press, 1959), pp.143-153, quoted in P.E. Vernon, ed., *Creativity*, p.133.

6. Ibid., p.134.

7. Ben Shahn, *The Shape of Content* (Cambridge: Harvard University Press, 1976), p.35.

8. Eduard Hanslick, *The Beautiful in Music* (Indianapolis: The Bobbs-Merrill Company, 1957), p.22.

9. Ibid., p.23.

10. Shahn, *Shape of Content*, p.50.

11. Popper, *Logic of Scientific Discovery*, p.31.

12. Ibid., p.32.

13. Hattiangadi, "Vanishing Context of Discovery."

14. Israel Scheffler, "Making and Understanding," in B. Arnstine and D. Arnstine, eds., *Philosophy of Education 1987* (Normal, Il.: Philosophy of Education Society, forthcoming.)

15. Ibid.

16. Maitland, "Creativity," p.397.

17. Scheffler, "Making and Understanding."

18. Robert Ennis, "A Conception of Rational Thinking," in J. Coombs, ed., *Philosophy of Education 1979* (Normal, Il, Philosophy of Education Society, 1980), p.5.

19. Michael Scriven, *Reasoning* (New York: McGraw-Hill, 1976), p.36.

20. Richard Paul, "Teaching Critical Thinking in the Strong Sense: A Focus on Self-Deception, World Views, and a Dialectical Mode of Analysis," *Informal Logic* 4, 2 (1982): 2-7.

21. David Perkins, "Reasoning as Imagination," in S. Bailin, D. Perkins, and I. Winchester, eds., *Creativity, Education and Thought, Interchange* 16, 1 (1985): 15-16.

22. Israel Scheffler, "Philosophical Models in Teaching," in R.S. Peters, ed., *The Concept of Education* (London: Routledge and Kegan Paul, 1967), p.124.

23. Israel Scheffler, "In Praise of the Cognitive Emotions," in I. Scheffler, *Science and Subjectivity*, 2nd Edition (Indianapolis: Hackett Publishing Company, 1982).

24. R.S. Peters, "Reason and Passion," in R.F. Dearden, P.H. Hirst, and R.S. Peters, eds., *Education and the Development of Reason* (London: Routledge and Kegan Paul, 1972).

25. See Scheffler, "In Praise of the Cognitive Emotions," pp.143-145.

26. Ibid., p.156.

27. Peter McKellar, *Imagination and Thinking* (London: Cohen and West, 1957), p.116.

# INDEX

acting, 18, 93, 112, 116
actor, 112, 116
aesthetic appeal, 37
aesthetic emotion, 37, 47
aesthetic experience, 35, 48, 55
aesthetic judgment, 55
aesthetic qualities, 48
aesthetic response, 44, 47
algebra, 24
algorithm, 106
anomaly, 29
antecedent, 13
application, 22, 27, 43, 61, 62, 98, 105, 122, 127
appraisal, 53, 55, 102
appreciation, 37, 44, 46, 47, 55, 56, 58
arbitrary novelty, 31, 39, 109, 126, 131
architecture, 41, 42
**Aristotle**, 90, 106
art, 8, 9, 12, 13, 14, 16, 17, 18, 20, 27, 28, 29, 30, 33, 34, 35, 36, 37, 38, 39, 40, 41, 42, 43, 44, 45, 46, 47, 48, 49, 54, 55, 56, 57, 58, 59, 63, 64, 77, 78, 79, 83, 89, 90, 91, 92, 103, 109, 110, 111, 113, 115, 117, 118, 119, 120, 121, 122, 123
artist, 12, 28, 29, 30, 36, 37, 38, 40, 41, 48, 57, 70, 78, 79, 90, 91, 92, 95, 97, 110, 111, 113, 114, 115, 116, 117, 122, 123
assessment, 4, 18, 26, 33, 34, 35, 45, 49, 52, 53, 54, 61, 102, 103
assumption, 7, 34, 61, 69, 84, 86, 88, 92, 113
attention, 75, 96
attitude, 2, 128, 131

authenticity, 48
authority, 74, 81, 131
awareness, 87, 93, 95, 96, 127
**Bach**, 15, 31, 39, 111, 119
**Bacon**, 102
**Barron, F.**, 2, 5, 6, 86
**Beardsley, Monroe**, 77, 86, 106
beauty, 56
**Beckett, Samuel**, 29
**Bell, Clive**, 35, 36, 37, 38 59
**Birch**, 104
body of facts, 73, 130
boundary-breaking, 23
brainstorming, 66, 130
**Brecht**, 40
**Brown, Harold I**, 19, 32
**Browning, Robert**, 110
**Bruner, Jerome**, 74, 85, 124
**Camus**, 42
capacity, 62, 63, 64, 79, 82, 83, 84
category, 8, 9, 119
chance, 28, 29, 30, 67, 69, 83
choreography, 17, 18
cognition, 127
cognitive ability, 81
cognitive traits, 2
**Collingwood, R. G.**, 70, 78, 85, 86, 90, 91, 106, 122
communication, 9, 10
composer, 15, 17, 49, 115, 119, 123
composition, 114
conceptual language, 35
conceptual scheme, 99
concretization, 76, 77, 78
consciousness, 14, 34, 40, 92
**Constable**, 39
constraints, 4, 15, 16, 17, 18, 31, 58, 69, 75, 76, 92, 121

contemporary view, 3, 4, 5, 87, 104, 105, 106, 122, 128, 129, 131
context, 9, 10, 13, 22, 25, 26, 27, 28, 44, 45, 57, 68, 74, 81, 83, 84, 85, 87, 89, 97, 103, 107, 109, 121
context of discovery, 103, 107
continuity, 7, 13, 19, 54, 71, 99, 121
control, 91, 92, 95, 102, 116
convention, 17, 89, 93
**Copernican model**, 73
**Copernican view**, 73, 74
copy, 47, 48, 49, 57
craft, 11, 22, 90, 92, 122
creating, 1, 12, 13, 16, 17, 28, 30, 63, 64, 67, 70, 71, 74, 75, 76, 77, 78, 79, 80, 84, 85, 91, 92, 97, 102, 118, 122, 123, 129, 131
creation, 8, 11, 12, 13, 14, 16, 17, 23, 29, 30, 37, 57, 63, 64, 69, 70, 71, 72, 74, 76, 77, 78, 79, 85, 89, 90, 91, 98, 100, 102, 112, 113, 114, 117, 119, 121, 122, 123, 124, 127
creative act, 67, 68, 87
creative leaps, 73
creative person, 61, 84, 85
creative personality, 5, 61, 81, 82
creative potential, 79
creative process, 3, 5, 61, 64, 66, 67, 68, 71, 73, 76, 77, 84, 85, 91, 92, 128, 129
creative thinking, 2, 67, 74, 76
creative work, 10, 28, 109, 113, 117
creative writing, 117
creativity paradox, 91
critical thinking, 124, 125
criticism, 93, 121, 122, 124, 126, 130, 131
culture, 5, 10, 11, 28, 34, 82, 126, 131

**Cummings, e.e.**, 14
curiosity, 56, 128
dance, 17, 18, 88
dancer, 78, 88
**Darwin, C.**, 81, 82
data, 51, 82, 99, 102
deductive reasoning, 25
departure, 7, 16, 19, 20, 26, 44, 45, 68, 71, 89
development, 2, 5, 13, 18, 19, 24, 39, 40, 42, 45, 46, 56, 58, 94, 96, 99, 109, 115, 118, 129, 131
director, 16, 18, 112, 116
discipline, 4, 8, 20, 23, 24, 27, 34, 38, 39, 40, 44, 62, 76, 81, 82, 83, 96, 97, 105, 106, 122, 125, 129, 130
discontinuity, 3, 4, 7, 8, 10, 18, 52, 53, 59, 96, 99
divergence, 7, 17, 84
divergent thinking, 2, 74, 79, 80, 86, 99
**Dostoevsky, F.** 80
drama, 13, 16, 40, 42, 47
dream, 77, 78
drill, 94, 95
**Duchamp, M.** 9
education, 1, 2, 4, 7, 84
efficacy, 21, 25
**Einstein, A.**, 19, 20, 71, 80, 120
elaboration, 66
elegance, 23, 56
emotion, 14, 55, 91, 114, 115, 117, 118, 119, 127
environment, 74, 83
epistemology, 88
evaluation, 1, 3, 4, 15, 33, 34, 35, 38, 39, 41, 42, 45, 49, 52, 53, 54, 55, 59, 75, 95, 102, 103, 107, 120, 121, 122, 123, 124, 129
evaluative criteria, 53
evidence, 31, 50, 51, 53, 55, 58, 62, 74, 77, 79, 86, 100

evolution, 40, 43, 54, 82, 87, 109, 125, 128, 129, 130, 131
excellence, 4, 89
execution, 15, 17, 22, 30, 32, 44, 48, 70, 78, 90, 109, 112, 114, 115, 122, 123
experience, 25, 35, 37, 47, 50, 70, 72, 87, 88, 101, 104, 105, 111, 117, 118
experiment, 50, 51, 68, 70, 92
experimentation, 29, 50
expertise, 47, 67, 95, 97, 105, 106, 114
explanation, 5, 30, 46, 50, 53, 58, 67, 74, 75, 124, 128
explanatory adequacy, 53
exploration, 7, 15, 21, 24, 31, 40, 45, 56, 67, 68, 121
expression, 7, 9, 14, 35, 36, 41, 90, 91, 92, 110, 111, 112, 115, 119
extraordinary achievement, 2
fact, 8, 10, 13, 22, 26, 27, 30, 31, 34, 35, 36, 42, 45, 46, 47, 48, 49, 50, 51, 52, 54, 55, 58, 59, 60, 61, 62, 63, 67, 71, 75, 77, 78, 81, 82, 87, 88, 90, 95, 96, 97, 99, 100, 102, 103, 104, 109, 114, 117, 119, 120, 127
falsificationism, 51
fantasy, 22, 116, 117
feeling, 35, 55, 56, 70, 75, 92, 112, 127
**Feyerabend, P.**, 34, 51, 52, 54, 59, 60, 87, 100, 101, 102, 106, 107
flexibility, 79, 84, 98, 99, 105, 121, 128, 130
fluency, 75, 76, 79, 80, 95, 128, 130
forehavings, 92, 123
foreknowledge, 91, 92, 122
foresight, 68, 91
forgery, 47, 48, 60
form, 9, 10, 13, 14, 15, 17, 21, 24, 25, 29, 31, 35, 36, 37, 38, 39, 40, 41, 42, 43, 45, 46, 52, 56, 63, 68, 69, 70, 74, 76, 87, 88, 89, 90, 98, 104, 116, 119, 120, 123, 128
fostering creativity, 128
framework, 3, 8, 9, 12, 14, 15, 18, 19, 23, 24, 26, 29, 38, 39, 40, 44, 45, 47, 52, 56, 58, 66, 71, 72, 73, 74, 87, 88, 89, 98, 99, 101, 104, 113, 116, 117, 121
free play, 121, 122
freedom, 4, 38, 41, 94, 105, 122
**Freud, S.**, 30, 32, 86, 117, 118, 119 132
fruitfulness, 102
**Gainsborough, T.** 31
**Galileo**, 50, 73, 74, 85
**Gardner, H.**, 81, 86
generation, 3, 46, 64, 71, 77, 91, 102, 103, 106, 107, 109, 120, 121, 122, 123, 124, 127, 128, 129
genius, 1, 27, 33, 48, 89, 109
genre, 12, 13, 14, 15, 44, 88
geometry, 24
gestalt switch, 51, 52
goals, 13, 43, 45, 49, 56, 91, 95, 97, 130
**Gombrich, E. H.**, 41, 57, 60, 115, 131
**Goodman, N.**, 55, 60
gravitation, 19
**Guilford, J. P.**, 2, 5
habit, 3, 66, 87, 93, 94
**Handel**, 15
**Hanslick, E.**, 119, 132
**Hardy, T.**, 40
**Harlow**, 105
**Hattiangadi, J.**, 19, 32, 103, 107, 121, 132
**Hausman, C.**, 7, 31, 33, 59, 106
history, 10, 13, 18, 20, 38, 39, 44, 100, 126

**Howard, V.**, 68, 70, 78, 85, 86, 91, 93, 95, 106, 107
hypothesis, 20, 50
**Ibsen**, 14
illumination, 76, 77, 109
imagination, 2, 3, 5, 7, 22, 23, 30, 48, 49, 57, 61, 83, 91, 98, 109, 110, 111, 112, 113, 114, 115, 116, 117, 118, 119, 120, 121, 122, 124, 125, 128, 129, 131
**Impressionist**, 39, 56
improvement, 11, 21, 22, 58, 94, 126
incommensurability, 101
incubation, 76, 77
induction, 51
inductive inference, 50, 53
inductive reasoning, 49
inductivist account, 50
informal reasoning, 124
innovation, 7, 8, 9, 10, 13, 14, 16, 18, 20, 22, 23, 24, 29, 33, 34, 39, 44, 46, 71, 82, 89, 92, 96, 98, 116, 126, 130
inquiry, 20, 56, 125, 126, 127, 128, 130, 131
insight, 14, 27, 73, 74, 75, 76, 77, 78, 79, 104, 110, 111, 112, 115
inspiration, 1, 29, 56, 89, 90, 91, 95, 109, 110, 119, 122
intelligence, 122
intention, 28, 29, 30, 68, 70, 83, 123
interpretation, 16, 17, 18, 37, 59, 83, 111, 112, 114, 116
intuition, 120, 126, 127
invention, 21, 22, 24, 41, 42, 68, 100, 120, 121, 125
inventor, 21, 28
irrational process, 102
irrationality, 52, 130

**James, H.**, 14
**James, William**, 93, 107
**Joyce**, 14, 40
judgment, 3, 9, 16, 47, 55, 67, 68, 69, 70, 71, 72, 76, 80, 92, 94, 95, 96, 97, 98, 105, 109, 113, 115, 116, 117, 120, 121, 122, 124, 127, 129, 130, 131
**Kagan J.**, 28, 29, 32
**Kant, Immanuel**, 59
**Khatchadourian, H.**, 77, 86
knowledge, 3, 5, 7, 23, 24, 28, 36, 38, 44, 47, 50, 60, 68, 72, 88, 91, 95, 100, 103, 104, 105, 106, 116, 122, 125, 126, 128, 129, 130, 131
**Koestler, A.**, 64, 67, 82, 85, 86, 87, 93, 106, 107
**Kris, Ernst**, 38, 59
**Kuhn, T.**, 7, 18, 19, 31, 32, 34, 51, 53, 54, 57, 58, 59, 60, 99, 107
**Lakatos, I.**, 50, 60
**Langer, S.**, 35, 59
lateral thinking, 66
**Leonardo**, 30, 32, 118
literature, 2, 13, 14, 36, 40, 42, 43, 75, 111, 115, 119
logical thinking, 5, 61, 66, 67, 128
**MacKinnon, D. W.**, 2, 5, 81, 86
**Mahler**, 119
**Maitland, J.**, 78, 86, 92, 106, 107, 123, 132
mastery, 15, 38, 39, 94, 96, 105, 106, 111, 113
mathematician, 71
mathematics, 23, 24, 125
**McKellar, P.**, 131
measurement, 1
mechanization, 97, 130
medium, 9, 11, 12, 41, 63, 68, 90, 123
mental health, 84

mental process, 62
merit, 11, 17
meta-criteria, 54, 58, 102
meta-rules, 102, 103, 106
methodology, 4, 35, 51, 59
**Michelangelo**, 46, 114
**Miller, Arthur I.**, 20, 32
**Mondrian**, 111, 119
**Mozart, W. A.**, 15, 28, 29, 32
music, 14, 15, 16, 17, 39, 40, 41, 42, 43, 44, 47, 49, 74, 78, 97, 111, 112, 115, 119
**Newton, I.**, 19, 103
non-conformity, 81, 128
normal science, 18, 19, 58, 99
norms, 7, 11
novelty, 3, 4, 7, 8, 12, 13, 14, 15, 18, 21, 25, 26, 28, 33, 72, 80, 91, 128, 129
objective basis, 34
objective criteria, 4, 33, 34, 49, 51, 52, 59
objective evaluation, 52
objective standards, 45, 49, 54
objectivity, 55
observation, 1, 15, 49, 50, 101
open-ended problem, 26
ordinary language, 35
ordinary thinking, 3, 71, 76, 87
originality, 3, 4, 7, 8, 10, 11, 12, 13, 14, 15, 16, 17, 18, 20, 21, 22, 23, 24, 25, 26, 27, 28, 29, 30, 31, 84, 87
origination, 109
painting, 9, 11, 12, 14, 28, 33, 35, 36, 37, 39, 41, 42, 43, 47, 48, 57, 60, 63, 88, 91, 92, 98, 111, 114, 119
paradigm, 7, 18, 19, 51, 53, 57, 58, 99, 120, 121
**Parnes, S.**, 2, 6
**Parsons, M. J.**, 61, 62, 63, 64, 82, 83, 85, 86

**Patrick, C.**, 76, 77, 86
**Paul, R.**, 59, 85, 124, 132
pedagogical practice, 5
pedagogy, 7
perceptual shift, 104, 106
performance, 16, 17, 47, 49, 64, 89, 93, 94, 98, 105, 112
performing arts, 48, 112, 115
**Perkins, D. N.**, 70, 71, 74, 75, 76, 80, 85, 86, 125, 132
personal growth, 84
personality development, 4
personality traits, 1, 3, 61, 81, 82, 128, 129, 130
philosophy of science, 100, 103
photography, 9, 41, 42
physics, 20, 27, 71, 74, 82
**Picasso**, 12, 13, 28, 29, 33
planning, 90
**Plato**, 1, 5, 89, 90, 106
play, 16, 17, 29, 30, 36, 39, 40, 43, 45, 48, 49, 54, 56, 66, 70, 98, 103, 105, 110, 112, 114, 115, 116, 118, 122, 125, 127
playwright, 49
poet, 1, 63, 70, 71, 72, 75, 88, 115
poetry, 1, 14, 35, 63, 70, 72, 78, 90
**Polanyi, M.**, 98, 107
**Popper, K.**, 51, 60, 102, 107, 120, 132
portrayal, 13, 16, 42, 93, 114
possibilities, 16, 17, 18, 21, 22, 25, 26, 28, 33, 39, 41, 44, 45, 56, 57, 58, 67, 70, 71, 72, 89, 96, 98, 103, 109, 112, 116
**Poussin**, 12
practice, 1, 2, 4, 18, 19, 20, 23, 51, 52, 54, 66, 87, 95, 96, 98, 99, 100, 101, 106, 128
preconception, 69, 91

predecessor, 58
premature closure, 75
preparation, 66, 76
preselection, 71
presupposition, 19, 68, 71, 73
principle, 111
problems, 4, 7, 13, 14, 19, 20, 22, 23, 24, 25, 26, 28, 31, 35, 38, 39, 40, 43, 45, 50, 51, 53, 54, 56, 57, 58, 59, 61, 64, 66, 71, 73, 74, 75, 79, 101, 105, 106, 107, 113, 116, 120, 121, 122, 123, 125, 126, 128, 129, 130
problem-solving, 22, 25, 26, 66, 72, 84, 104, 105, 106, 113, 116
procedure, 25, 52, 53, 74, 77, 101, 102, 122
proficiency, 94, 96, 111, 113, 114
progress, 29, 52, 56, 57, 58, 71, 75, 88, 99, 100, 101
proof, 50
psychological tests, 64
quality, 1, 35, 39, 61, 76, 80, 111, 130, 131
radical change, 7, 19, 99
**Rameau**, 15
random elements, 29, 30
random happenings, 30
random stimulation, 66, 69, 70, 130
**Raphael**, 38, 110, 113, 114
rationality, 34, 49, 103, 122, 126, 127
**Read, H.**, 35, 59
realism, 89
receptivity, 128, 131
representation, 12, 35, 42, 49, 57
restructuring, 104
revision, 105, 121
revolutionary change, 26
rigidity, 3, 25, 66, 97, 130

rule-breaking, 3, 5, 61, 88, 89, 105, 109, 128, 130, 131
rules: of method, 87, 100, 101, 106
**Ryle, G.**, 93, 107
**Scheffler, I.**, 59, 93, 94, 107, 122, 123, 126, 127, 128, 132, 133
**Schumann**, 119
science, 2, 7, 18, 19, 20, 22, 23, 24, 34, 49, 51, 52, 53, 54, 55, 56, 57, 58, 59, 78, 87, 98, 99, 100, 102, 103, 105, 120, 121, 122
science fiction, 22, 23
scientific change, 20
scientific discovery, 18, 20, 78, 86, 98, 99, 100, 101, 102, 103, 105, 106, 121
scientific language, 35
scientific problem, 80
scientific research, 19
scientific theory, 50
scientist, 29, 38, 82, 98, 99, 120
**Scriven, M.**, 124, 132
sculpture, 12
seeing as, 111, 114
sensibility, 36, 37, 41, 42, 44, 45, 46, 55
**Shahn, B.**, 118, 119, 132
**Siegel, H.**, 53, 59, 60, 107
significance, 4, 18, 23, 31, 35, 36, 39, 45, 46, 59, 129
significant achievement, 1, 97, 109, 129, 131
simplicity, 43, 56, 102, 111
skill, 3, 5, 15, 23, 44, 48, 66, 70, 76, 80, 90, 93, 94, 95, 96, 109, 110, 111, 113, 114, 115, 116, 117, 119, 120, 121, 122, 127, 129, 130, 131
**Socrates**, 89
solution, 20, 23, 24, 25, 26, 27, 29, 54, 57, 66, 67, 68, 69, 102, 104, 105, 120, 125

something more, 3, 83, 109, 111, 112, 113, 115, 116, 117, 120
**Sparshott, F.**, 117, 132
spectator, 37, 117, 119, 120
spontaneity, 68, 84, 91
stages, 29, 76, 77, 78, 79
standards, 3, 11, 19, 33, 34, 49, 51, 52, 53, 54, 55, 58, 76, 93, 113, 116, 130
strategy, 26, 95, 105
**Stravinsky, I.**, 15, 39, 60
style, 11, 12, 18, 29, 31, 33, 38, 39, 41, 44, 56, 83, 88, 113, 116, 117
subconscious, 30, 118, 119
subject matter, 11, 12, 14, 15, 29, 30, 42, 43, 66, 130
subjective factors, 33, 52, 54, 56, 59
subjective preference, 45
subjective response, 47
subjectivist account, 54
subjectivist position, 34, 45, 46, 49
subjectivity, 59
surprise, 28, 29, 123, 127, 128
suspension of judgment, 3, 61, 66, 67, 71, 129
symbol, 118
symbolic logic, 24
talent, 83
technique, 12, 14, 28, 40, 41, 44, 53, 69, 70, 88, 90, 91, 102, 113, 116, 118
technology, 9, 22, 23, 40, 41, 42
testing, 49, 53, 79, 80, 100, 123
theatre, 16, 40, 43, 89
theatrical arts, 112
theorem, 24
theory of relativity, 19, 42, 71, 120
thinking process, 2, 25
thought process, 62
**Tomas, V.**, 85, 91, 106, 107
**Torrance, E. P.**, 1, 2, 5, 6
tradition, 4, 7, 8, 9, 13, 14, 18, 20, 28, 31, 33, 34, 35, 38, 39, 40, 44, 45, 46, 49, 54, 59, 82, 88, 99, 100, 106, 116, 126, 131
training, 69, 93, 94
transformation, 54, 114
truth, 56, 57, 58, 73, 127
unconscious factors, 30, 118
unconscious processes, 67, 74, 77
understanding, 5, 10, 13, 23, 27, 45, 46, 56, 58, 75, 94, 97, 103, 110, 112, 119, 126, 130, 131
uniqueness, 12, 80
value, 3, 11, 26, 31, 33, 34, 35, 36, 37, 38, 39, 40, 41, 43, 44, 45, 46, 47, 48, 49, 52, 54, 55, 56, 57, 62, 83, 93
verification, 66, 76, 78, 127
vertical thinking, 66
vision, 30, 40, 78, 90, 109, 111, 113, 114, 115, 116, 120
**Vivaldi**, 15
**Wallas, G.**, 76, 77, 86
**Weisberg, D.**, 74, 76, 85, 86, 104, 105, 107
**White, J. P.**, 61, 62, 63, 82, 83, 85, 86
**Williams, T.**, 118